With Love
and Laughter,

With Love
and Laughter,

John Ritter

AMY YASBECK

GALLERY BOOKS
New York London Toronto Sydney

G

Gallery Books
A Division of Simon & Schuster, Inc.
1230 Avenue of the Americas
New York, NY 10020

Copyright © 2010 by Amy Yasbeck

First Gallery Books hardcover edition September 2010

GALLERY BOOKS and colophon are trademarks
of Simon & Schuster, Inc.

For information about special discounts for bulk purchases, please contact Simon & Schuster Special Sales at 1-866-506-1949 or business@simonandschuster.com.

The Simon & Schuster Speakers Bureau can bring authors to your live event. For more information or to book an event contact the Simon & Schuster Speakers Bureau at 1-866-248-3049 or visit our website at www.simonspeakers.com.

Lyrics to "Hurt" by Trent Reznor used by permission.

Designed by Jaime Putorti

Manufactured in the United States of America

10 9 8 7 6 5 4 3 2 1

Library of Congress Cataloging-in-Publication Data
Yasbeck, Amy.
    With love and laughter, John Ritter / by Amy Yasbeck.
        p. cm.
    1. Ritter, John. 2. Television actors and actresses—United States—Biography. 3. Motion picture actors and actresses—United States—Biography. I. Title.
    PN2287.R545Y37 2010
    791.4502'8092—dc22
    [B]   2010011346

ISBN 978-1-4165-9854-1

For Stella

contents

Contents

John Ritter's Window

John died the night of September 11, 2003. Not only was it our daughter Stella's fifth birthday but it was only a few days into her first real week of school. In fact, it was the first day that we parents were expected to drop our kids off instead of walking them in and hovering.

I think the thing with which children and their parents comfort themselves is the knowledge that these separations last only a few hours. Moms and dads reassure their little ones that they will be back for them, even though most parents feel in the pit of their stomachs that they're kind of abandoning them—especially if it's their first kid and/or only one. I remember seeing parents and their kids dotting the campus in little intimate clumps, basically having the same conversation: "We'll be back for you. It's just a few hours—you'll have a lot of fun and it'll go by before you know it."

Stella had gone to a small co-op nursery school for the previous two years. Co-op, mind you, means that the parents work at school, so John and I were there a lot. This whole kindergarten thing on a giant campus at a big school that went up to eighth grade was a really different feeling for all of us. It was like trying to merge onto an L.A. freeway driving a Big Wheel. As a brand-new five-year-old, Stella was as brave and trusting of the world—and of us—as we could have hoped. She shared a good-bye kiss with her father that morning believing, on faith, that her time at school would be bookended by another kiss at the end of her day. She'll never have that kiss.

Late that afternoon, John was taken from work to the emergency room of the hospital across the street. I rushed there to be with him. He died hours later. Stella never saw him again.

Every five-year-old's nightmare, whether they can verbalize it or not, is that when they say good-bye to their parents, their parents disappear. Good-bye is good-bye. No differentiation between "good-bye see you later" and "good-bye forever." This nightmare came true for Stella. I know kids live through this. I've met plenty of adults who lost a parent very, very young. But you can never imagine, until it happens to you, what it's like to witness your child's suffering. As much pain as I was in, trying to wrap my head and heart around my own loss, nothing will ever compare with the absolute despair of experiencing this tragedy through my daughter's eyes.

My first instinct was to keep her out of school and hibernate the rest of the year away; she could just start again the next September. I knew this was the wrong tack and I would have to pull her out of school for a while and then slowly re-introduce her to the idea of kindergarten. After a pretty cruel false start, it wasn't going to be easy. Besides, John was the big school fan. He loved school, everything about it. He had an abundance of warm memories about his adventures in grade school and at his beloved Hollywood High and USC.

Me? Not so much. My experiences were not so nice. John and I had an understanding that he was going to be holding my hand for the next twelve or so years when it came to anything school-related. I was in this alone now and everyone's advice that September was that Stella needed school and normalcy . . . right. Okay.

One week after John died, Stella started back at school. The drill was: I would go to school with her, drop her off in class, hang around close by, and then slowly start to leave campus for longer and longer periods of time. Clearly, this was as hard for me as it was for her. Her school was up on Mulholland Drive. And when I first forced myself to get back in my car and actually drive away from her, I didn't get very far. In fact, I just drove in huge loops down to Ventura Boulevard, slowly cruising along for a couple of miles, then back up another canyon to Mulholland, across the tops of the mountains past her school, and then back down another canyon road to Ventura Boulevard in the Valley.

I didn't listen to the radio. Not only was talk radio to be avoided—especially Howard Stern—but every song was about John. When I was pregnant with Stella, he told me that one of the many amazing effects that having a baby has on your relationship to the world is that every song on the radio becomes about your baby. Every love song is suddenly about your new love. This little person.

It's true for every parent. I remember my dad, who sang me to sleep every night with a repertoire of songs from the thirties and forties, his era, used to effortlessly replace the word "baby" with "Amy." As in, "just Dorothy and me and Amy makes three, we're happy in our blue heaven." Now here I was driving radio-free, testing the radius of my invisible umbilical cord; all the songs were about John now. Just the thought of music, any song, made me cry so hard my glasses would fog up. Unsafe at any speed.

At some point during that first week back at school, I decided to widen my comfort zone by taking a longer drive down Ventura Boulevard before I climbed back up the mountain on the way to Stella's school. I found myself at the stretch between Jerry's Deli and The Good Earth Restaurant, two of John and Stella and my favorites. This was worse than being blindsided by a Beatles song. My face flushed and my glasses fogged and I had to pull over. I happened to have stopped in front of a newsstand. I had purposely been avoiding headlines. No TV. No Internet. Nothing. I should have been expecting some stories about John to show up in the gossip magazines, but I certainly wasn't seeking them out. And, thankfully, I had been surrounded by friends and family kind enough to keep any knowledge of press coverage to themselves.

As I glanced up at the newsstand, a big, bold headline caught my eye: JOHN RITTER'S WINDOW COLLAPSES. I was thinking, *Holy crap, now what? His dressing room window over at Disney?* I pulled down my Dodgers cap—actually,

John's Dodgers cap that he had given me to hold with his watch and wallet and wedding ring that night in the emergency room. I really did not want to be recognized. Nobody wants to be spotted reading the rags. I got out of the car and stood about ten feet away from the magazine rack in an attempt to appear nonchalant, nearly backing into traffic in the process.

JOHN RITTER'S WINDOW COLLAPSES—maybe it was a concocted story about a window at our house? Under the headline was a photo of us from some event. I inched up to get a closer look at this picture that I had never seen before. John standing behind me with his hand on my shoulders, smiling. It hit me like a throat punch. Not "window." *Widow.*

The reality sat me down right where I stood, literally. I didn't cry. I didn't panic. I just sat there on the curb and took in the events of the last week in one bitter gulp and let it move through me. Past my skin, into my gut. I felt it settle like a flock of birds somewhere around where my heart sat seemingly motionless in my chest, waiting for permission to beat again.

The reality of my new label took up residence in the center of my being. JOHN RITTER'S WIDOW COLLAPSES. Define "collapse." Nothing in the article was true. And yet having the W-word used in reference to me was truth enough. Even though John and I had been together a long time, we had been married for only four years. I was still getting butterflies every time he or anyone else would use the other W-word, wife. I'm sure the word "widow" was all over the place in reference to me. I just didn't feel it—own it—until then.

When I was a little girl, my friends and I would play with our baby dolls outside in our yards. Thinking back, none of us really felt comfortable pretending to be single moms. It was the end of the sixties, beginning of the seventies, and even though we didn't know what the concern was exactly, we knew there was something troubling about it. We would start every session of playing house by explaining to one another where our husbands were. Usually everyone just said "at work."

I remember being with my friends one day in my side yard beneath our famous crabapple tree (famous because of my mom's applesauce and apple jelly). On this particular afternoon, our imaginations extended past the daytime housewife hours and we all seemed to be living with our babies in some kind of kibbutz. We were gathering food for them when one of the girls announced that her husband had gotten killed in Vietnam and wasn't coming home. There was a heavy pause and then the other girls began to nod knowingly and commiserate that they, too, had lost their husbands to the controversial war in Vietnam. I remember the little war widows looking at me expectantly. I couldn't even say the words. Even then I couldn't quite *go there*.

"He's an astronaut," I said. "He'll be away for a couple years, and then he'll be back." I assured them that the baby and I were fine. I remember that like it was yesterday.

I think that's where I was for a long time after John died. That's the kind of place I would go when uninterrupted by condolences or tributes or Stella's innocent but brutally stark questions. It wasn't exactly denial or mental illness or some kind of veiled religiosity. My head game was survival, pure and simple.

The only way I could take a step or a breath, much less go about the business of living, was to cling to the closest recognizable feeling I could handle. At night, all hell would break loose inside my head. And my heart would break over and over and over. But in the morning, after the initial slap in the face that every new awakening would bring, I would drift into survival mode. I allow myself to believe that this was all just a crazy extended version of all the brief times apart that John and I had already survived.

So familiar, this waiting. Over our years together I'd had so many tastes of it. The anticipation, the romantic longing, the resenting everyone for not being John. Then just when I was sure I would lose my mind: the crashing together and making up and out for lost time. I knew in my heart I wasn't going to get my way this time. I wanted to hold my breath till I turned blue . . . I am blue now. Was all of that a rehearsal for this?

With Love
and Laughter,

chapter 1

America's Most Beloved
Cowboy's Most Beloved Son's Brother

I always saw it coming, but it got me every time. Some poor schmo would innocently ask John if his late father, singing cowboy star Tex Ritter, was actually from Texas. Without fail, John would answer, "Actually, he was born in Louisiana, but he figured Louise Ritter might not pack the same punch." The smartass comeback, lifted directly from his father's act, always got a laugh.

John had show business in his blood. His mother, Dorothy Fay Southworth, was a gorgeous, talented, vivacious young woman with acting aspirations of her own. After studying theater at the Royal Academy of Dramatic Art in London, she moved to Hollywood, where she did her fair share of print work as a model while auditioning for films. After her big break, screen testing with Alan Ladd, she was offered a contract with 20th Century Fox studio. Soon after, her father in Prescott, Arizona, became ill. The decision to stay with her dying father would mean losing her opportunity to be a contract player with the studio. She chose to turn her back on her contract and stay by her father's side. Dorothy went on to be cast in several movies, one of which was *Rainbow Over the Range,* starring opposite Tex Ritter. They starred in a few more movies, and then spent the rest of their lives together.

Tex and his brothers and sisters had been raised on a farm in East Texas with lots of animals. They all learned to ride horses as little children. Even as a youngster, Tex immersed himself in the history and traditions of the Old West. His passion for storytelling and music would eventually spin him into a career in show business—he became a singing cowboy. He made sixty-five movies in twenty years, from 1936 to 1956. He was a movie star and also made dozens and dozens of albums. Not long after his sons, Tom and John, were born in 1947 and 1948, his movies were rerunning on Saturday morning television. Dorothy would yell "Dad's on!" and the boys would race to the TV to watch their father singing, courting, riding, and fighting.

In John's estimation, Tex was one of the best stage fighters the silver screen had ever seen. When most kids were singing into a hairbrush in front of the mirror, doing their best Elvis imitation, John was intently studying his father's every move. As a kid, through college, and for the rest of his life, John would entertain everyone with his famous "fight the invisible man" bit. He would throw and receive punches with astonishing believability. All by himself.

John was the baby of his family and was, by all accounts, a goofball from the beginning. The thing that's key about entertainers in general and John in particular is the ability to connect, to absorb, and to reflect the human condition. His powers of observation and mimicry expressed themselves early on, much to the delight of every student, and a few of the teachers, who found themselves in class with him. He could capture the essence of a person and present it back to them in an original way that was fascinating and revealing. John's interpretations of people and situations were simultaneously familiar and revelatory. He had clearly inherited the performance gene.

When John was two years old, his brother was diagnosed with cerebral palsy. While the boys were growing up, their parents' attention was, understandably, focused mainly on Tommy. Even as an adult John would launch into hilarious good-natured rants enumerating the iniquities of growing up in their house as an able-bodied kid. Those of us who knew John knew that when he was "making light" he was also shedding light. After one such extended recounting of his father's habit of punishing him even when his brother messed up, I decided to rename John. Inspired by Tex Ritter's moniker as "America's Most Beloved Cowboy," I dubbed John "America's Most Beloved Cowboy's Most Beloved Son's Brother." He took it well. Despite the perception on John's part of what he regarded as unequal treatment, the brothers developed a perfect bond. Undoubtedly, their shared experience growing up as Tex and Dorothy's boys gave them a unique perspective that only the two of them could truly understand.

John told me that it was very easy to be respectful to his dad. "After you've watched your dad beat the crap out of

Charlie King or some other bad guy in about forty movies, you pretty much always said, 'Yes, sir,' and meant it." No one ever really explained their dad's movies to them, so they thought that all of his adventures as a Texas Ranger really happened. Tex was their father but he was also a hero to them, as were Hopalong Cassidy and Roy Rogers.

John and Tom were living the dream of a lot of little boys in those days. Most of their peers were cowboy fans, but *they* got to live with the real thing. And Tex *was* the real thing. He wore the clothes and the boots and topped off the look with a cowboy hat. John used to say, "Dad didn't wear the guns unless a report card came in that he didn't particularly dig."

He loved to travel the country and perform for live audiences. In describing his dad's touring experience, John used to reference the movie *Coal Miner's Daughter*, for which Sissy Spacek won a well-deserved Oscar for her portrayal of Loretta Lynn. Just like in the movie, Tex would perform on a little stage in a flatbed truck with Christmas lights thrown up for ambience. He wanted to play music and sing and tell stories to the real folks, so he brought his act to people who would not have been able to make it to one of his more highfalutin venues.

An unquenchable curiosity about the Old West fed Tex's desire to travel the country and swap stories with ranchers and cowboys and everyday people. Dorothy and the boys would often accompany him and his band in the summers. Tex, a Civil War scholar, pointed out landmarks and waxed historic, while his sons, engrossed in their comics, threw in the occasional "Hmm." He would point out the station wagon window and explain in his signature commanding tone: "General Tecumseh Sherman died on that rock there, right after he fired a musket and hit Beauregard Jones in the nose. Boys, could you lift up your faces from the comic book and look out the window?"

Their father's history lessons not only had to compete with the adventures of Superman, but perhaps even more distracting were the sounds emanating from the band bus. Uproarious laughter and wild screams could be heard from the wild guys rocking out to country music, doing God knows what. Certainly, John and Tom did not know what. This was many years before Tex had sat the boys down when they were fifteen and sixteen and said, "Your mother wants me to talk to you and your brother about sex." John said, "Dad, if there's anything you want to know, come to me, feel free." By John's account, his sassy comeback had the desired effect. Tex was definitely thrown for a moment. After hemming and hawing uncharacteristically for a few minutes, he summed up his "birds and bees" talk by advising John: "Son, for now, you just use that little tallywhacker there for peeing through."

In 1954, Tex Ritter and Johnny Cash opened at The Showboat Casino in Las Vegas. The little Ritter boys got to spend time with Johnny and his band. When Bob Dylan made *Nashville Skyline* in 1965, Johnny Cash wrote the liner notes and sang "Girl from the North Country" with him. It was Bob Dylan's first foray from folk music into country and western. John said his friends were asking one another, "Have you heard this new guy Johnny Cash? He's so cool." And he would pipe up with, "He knows me. He opened for my dad ten years ago in Vegas and he calls me Johnathan. Do I know Johnny Cash? I hang with Johnny Cash."

Tex ran into financial trouble after his unsuccessful run in Tennessee for a seat in the U.S. Senate in 1970. Howard Baker wanted him to run as a moderate Republican against the conservative candidate. Tex was left with a lot of debt after his defeat. But Johnny Cash, out of the kindness of his heart, put together a benefit with some of his friends to help pay off Tex's campaign debt. John was truly touched by his generosity and always loved Johnny for being a true friend to his dad. In Nashville on September 12, 2003, Johnny Cash passed away. His death came just hours after John's, doubling the world's grief at the loss of these two talented and irreplaceable men.

Tex was the first president of the Country Music Association. In 1974, he got in touch with the great American painter Thomas Hart Benton and commissioned a mural for the Country Music Hall of Fame depicting the roots of country and western music. In the six-by-ten-foot oil painting, the artist pays homage to the disparate elements of American music that comprise the pastiche that has come to be known as country music. Benton honors the musical melting pot by portraying figures representing gospel music, railroad music, and spirituals. He included a joyous cowboy, head thrown back, singing straight up at the sky. He pointed this guitar-playing figure out to John's dad and said, "This is you, Tex."

The distinctive painting now hangs in the Country Music Hall of Fame in Nashville. In 1995, John was asked to host Tennessee's statehood bicentennial celebration. From the time our plane touched down, there was no doubt that our first stop would be the Country Music Hall of Fame, as John was very anxious to show me the painting. He gave me an incredible insider's tour. John had an amazing memory . . . when he chose to use it. On that day, he seemed to remember every story his father and mother had told him about the early days of country and western music. And when he showed me Benton's painting, I could have stood in front of it all day, drinking it in, marveling at its complex simplicity, or its simple complexity. One of the most interesting things about the painting is what is *not* there. Unlike the rest of Benton's work, there was no signature. John explained that after the completion of the painting, Benton's wife went out to her husband's art studio only to find him in front of the mural, dead, with his paintbrush still in his hand. The brush had been dipped in black paint, and it was still wet. He had died right before signing his final masterpiece.

John and his family treasured the mural because it depicts American music, like America herself, as enormous, diverse, and strengthened both by our unique experiences and our common heart.

John's eclectic musical tastes developed steadily throughout his life. His friends and family came to expect a musical experience whenever DJ Dad was driving. He shared his love of artists old and new with anyone who would listen. Stella was the one who asked me, just days after John died, to make sure we saved all of the music from his car. Numbly, I collected dozens of discs from his glove box and backseat. As an afterthought, I turned on the ignition and fumbled with the CD player in an attempt to eject whatever may have been in there. I accidentally hit *play* and all at once Johnny Cash's beautiful, mournful voice was singing to me. His cover of "Hurt" is about looking back at a journey's end. It was the song John had been listening to on his last morning here.

If I could start again
A million miles away
I would keep myself
I would find a way

~Trent Reznor

chapter 2

....

Caboose

In 1962, I was born into an already well-established family. I don't mean "established" in the social, dynastic sense, but "established" in the sense that they would have been just fine without me. Like the bread basket showing up after dessert, it was as if life's busboy misunderstood my father's "Can you please ask our waitress to bring our check" gesture and accidentally started the whole meal over.

My parents, John and Dorothy Yasbeck, had four kids: Ann, Rex, Patti, and Jay. At eighteen, sixteen, fourteen, and twelve, my siblings were more than content with the size of their family and their kick-ass border collie, Skippy. They probably weren't begging for a baby sister. But these things happen. They happen even when your parents have Ricky and Lucy Ricardo–style twin beds separated by a four-foot space. The span was temptingly dangerous enough to claim me as a victim when, at five (seven years before Evel Kneivel's Snake River Canyon jump), I attempted to leap it and busted my tailbone. Thankfully, my dad had succeeded in his attempt to brave the divide. Go, Dad. My father was always ready with a story, a joke, or an opinion, and never failed to enlighten, challenge, validate, and entertain me.

He taught himself American history. We had a gold couch from Ethan Allen with little white American eagles embroidered into the upholstery. My dad would lie on it in the oddest position with a washcloth under his head, because my mom didn't want him to get VO5 on the arm of the couch, and read every book about American history he could get his hands on. Even now I watch the History Channel for two, still learning and gathering information and stories to share with him even though he's been gone for years.

Dad shared his views on history with us kids, and his teachings didn't always go over well when we parroted them at school. My brother once piped up in class with: "My dad says George Washington was a traitor." "No, he was a patriot." "Well, it depends on how you look at it, because he had to be a traitor to someone." My dad got called in on that one.

His pool of knowledge was a fascinating amalgam of self-taught history and science, uncommon common sense, and unwavering devotion to Catholic dogma. He would have absolutely thrived in any university or seminary that would have been lucky enough to have him. Fortunately for all of us, Dad's path took him from his native Canada to the U.S. Air Force, where he met our mother while stationed at Wright Air Force Base in Ohio. He went on to own and run our market, which was his family's trade. I always felt he played out his unrealized collegiate personality with us. He engaged all of us in discussion and encouraged debate (but always made sure that he won). The rare occasion when he would concede to me, by admitting, "Amy, you've got a point," would immediately be followed with: "But if you comb your hair just right, no one will ever know it's there." I certainly learned not to get too cocky.

Dad sang me to sleep every night until I was in second grade. I know all the songs from the thirties and forties, including quite a few of Tex Ritter's early hits. Dad would hold the skin in front of his throat and wiggle it over his Adam's apple to affect the appropriate Tex Ritter vibrato.

My mom did not sing. She smoked . . . elegantly. My dad managed to both smoke and sing simultaneously. I remember lying in bed and tracking the red glow of their lit cigarettes, as they waited for me to fall asleep. I know that these days, that brings to mind a horrible politically incorrect image. But to me cigarettes were just extensions of my parents, glowing and ever present. Like E.T.'s fingertip. In the morning they would always be back in their twin beds. I was never aware of them leaving me.

I lived in Ohio until I was nineteen and every time summer rolled around, I spent at least half of my nights sleeping on our screened-in porch. There are a few golden hours in the middle of the night in southern Ohio when the humidity is imperceptible. Every once in a while, even in the last few years of my father's life, when I was home from college during the summer, Dad would hang out on the porch with me until I fell asleep. We would sing together loud enough for the crickets to take notice. They would quiet down during the songs in what was either rapt attention, curiosity, or, most likely, fear. At the end of each song the cricket cacophony would start again. It did not go unnoticed by my father or me that this was more than a little like the din of thunderous applause. We would usually sing until our repertoire was spent, or until the train across the way would rumble by around 1:00 a.m., signaling that it was time for the finale. We would trade verses of "South of the Border" and end with a lazy chorus of mournful "Ay-yay-yay-ays." As my dad would kiss me good night and grab his pack of Phillip Morris Unfiltered to go back in the house, the cricket applause would resume and continue until morning.

At the ripe old age of six, I got to dip my pinky toe into the showbiz world. My sister Patti was twenty at the time and was a successful local model. While at a photo shoot she caught wind of the fact that the photographer's next gig would be for Kenner toys. They were looking for a little girl to appear on the box for the 1969 version of the Easy-Bake Oven. Hello? Patti jumped on it and whipped out my first-grade school picture. Right, the two-by-two-inch headshot—bold move, considering the wallet-size photo portrayed an American mixed breed who seemed to have just declared "uncle" in a wrestling match with her hair(itage). While in line for the class photo—alphabetical order, mind you, so I had some time on my hands—I had spied plastic stork-shaped safety scissors and decided to show my bangs, once and for all, who was boss. "Who's your daddy?!" (Actually, my daddy was a charming Lebanese man, who passed on to me a great respect for world history, the love of feta cheese, and the freaking crazy hair gene, that's who!)

In what just may be the most perplexing casting mystery to date, I got the job. My recollection of the actual photo shoot is kind of a fuzzy. It was a blur of bright lights, tense whispering, and untouchable desserts being guarded and fussed over by professional pastry fluffers. My sharpest and best memory is of the flagrant early morning deception required to liberate me from school for the big day. Nothing will ever be as satisfying as the image of disapproving, tongue-clucking nuns whispering conspiratorially to one another, as my statuesque miniskirted sister whisked me off to my midmorning "doctor's appointment." Can't keep Doctor Showbiz waiting, now can we?

As a child, my overly dramatic side would occasionally rear its needy head. Invariably, my parents would comment, "You are such a little actress." I received it, as it was undoubtedly intended, as a mildly stinging pejorative, spewed in the same spirit as, "You look like a ragamuffin," or "Hurry up, Pokey." Among the handful of things that my parents loved to say about me was that everyone had to "walk on eggshells around me." This always confused the hell out of me, because that happened to be exactly how I felt about being with my mom. I was always walking on eggshells. It wasn't as if an unguarded moment of immature insensitivity on my part would have made my mother snap at me or dissolve into tears. It was bigger and way scarier than that. Mom was diagnosed with manic depression when I was seven. I always felt that there had to be some magical recipe that would cure her, stabilize her, reinvigorate her, and wake up the mother in her that I knew she wanted to be to me.

My mother would sporadically and unexpectedly fix me in her gaze and say what every young child should not hear: "I don't know what I would do without you." It sounded sweet to my ears, but as it would travel to my brain and then take its inevitable turn to the pit of my stomach, I would become painfully aware of its mass. In light of the other seemingly innocuous comments about me that were being haphazardly thrown around at the time—"Having Amy has saved Dorothy's life," or "Thank God your mom has you"—I was a hero complex waiting to happen.

All I knew was that I had been handed a task to which I was not equal. There is a certain backhanded powerlessness that comes with this kind of false sense of power. And this business of me having some higher purpose was especially confusing. I knew I was unplanned, yet I felt the same kind of weight of purpose that must be felt by children purposely conceived as bone marrow donors for their siblings must feel. Truth is, I would have gladly donated my bone marrow, my bones, or any transferable body part to save my mother from bipolar disorder, manic depression, freaking nuttiness—whatever we were calling it back then.

In my case, however, the recipe for avoiding disaster had nothing to do with harvesting or sharing. My particular mission statement was not as clear cut. It seemed like it had something to do with being perfect, which I clearly wasn't, or being a distraction, which I tried my best to be. It was a quest with no discernible goal. ("What is this Holy Grail of which you speak?" "You'll know it when you see it.") As a child, the only way for me to validate whether I was on the right track was to closely observe the barometer of my mother's moods. What part of bipolar did I not understand? Every part; I was seven.

My mother's mood was like the weather in Cincinnati: You don't like it? Wait a while. A while, in my mother's case, was a cycle usually consisting of about three years of normal to depressive, followed by a couple of months of queasy denial that an upward mood spike was on the horizon. Every once in a while there was some well-intentioned, mild interrogation of me. I was to keep an eye on my mother. To report on her: Did she leave cigarettes burning in every room? Was she making lists? Was she shopping too much? Was her speech fast and pressured? Was she making outlandish plans? Much of the time my mother confided her dreams and schemes to me with such girlish hopefulness that I would lay aside my duty. I would maintain this double-agent role as long as I could. I became adept at satisfying my craving for a mother-daughter bond by being her confidant, while keeping my family's suspicions at bay.

As I got older, I became all too aware of the pattern. Over the years, every time she would start her climb, I would feel comforted and then ultimately guilty. At this stage of her cycle, the last week or so prior to her being committed, my mother and I would engage in a psychological dance that was unfair to both of us, but couldn't be avoided. I would glean every moment of intimacy and bonding and willfully blur the more disturbing aspects of what she was saying and doing.

On her part, there were ever-increasing smiles (crazy),

compliments (effusive), and plans (impossible). On my part, there was intense cherry-picking and a conspiratorial partnership that, viewed through my denial-colored glasses, could pass for the relationship I always wanted. Inevitably, an innocent comment or grudging admission to my family would confirm that Mom was too ill not to be in the hospital. I came to associate telling the truth and betraying my mother's confidence with her being taken away from me. Though her debilitating cycle replayed itself for the rest of her life, I always knew that she loved me. Even in her most depressed state, I knew that she wanted me to be happy.

When I think of my mother now, I always remember our first conspiracy: her attempt to win one for Ireland. My father's swarthy genes had overpowered my mother's fair-haired variety at almost every turn. Out of the first four kids, my brother Jay ended up with her blue eyes, but aside from that isolated nod to the Emerald Isle, nothing. She knew that I, being fairly fair, was her last shot at having a kid who resembled her. Like every other child in the sixties, having my hair washed was pretty dull business. The choices were minimal: Johnson's Baby Shampoo and Prell were the go-to products in our house. One of us used Head & Shoulders, but why name names. Toward the end of my bath my mom would come in to assist me with the ole lather, rinse, repeat—but wait, there's more: She always squeezed lemon juice on my hair for the final step. I don't know how I knew, but I knew not to tell my dad our little "beauty secret." I was a strawberry blonde for a while there, though I'm not sure if it was due to genetics or the salad dressing in which I was being marinated nightly. Either way, the effect wore off in time and, like Jay, I ended up as a blue-eyed, dark-haired variety of Yasbeck.

Aside from a couple of misguided highlighting attempts in college, I never really messed around with my hair color. But after my mom passed away when I was twenty-one, I started to use a little henna every once in a while. "First one's free." Then I tried L'Oréal at home. "Because I was [pretending to be] worth it." Unbeknownst to me, L'Oréal is a gateway hair color. Soon I was hitting the hard stuff. Monthly appointments at salons. I never tried to kick it. Never considered going to red-hab.

I now feel like being untrue to my roots is a "tip of the hair" to my mom.

chapter 3

Mr. Ritter's Wild Ride

John began his professional acting career while he was still in college. As an undergraduate at the University of Southern California, he performed at the Edinburgh Theater Festival, acting in eighteen shows in three months. American television audiences saw him hundreds of times before they knew his name. In the seventies, he guest-starred on *Hawaii 5-0, Medical Center, M*A*S*H, The Streets of San Francisco, Kojak, The Mary Tyler Moore Show, Rhoda, Phyllis, Mannix,* and dozens more. "On-the-job training" was how John described his early acting career.

John's first film was *Scandalous John.* He had a small part but was determined to utilize his theater training. Having studied with such esteemed teachers as Mary Carver, Nina Foch, and Stella Adler, he was a very serious actor with a deep respect for the craft and was not about to merely show up on the set and take up space.

He was playing the role of the bad guy's lawyer and wanted to invest his character with true motivation. He decided to style his hair a different way, wear cufflinks and man jewelry, and make his face tight and hollow in an attempt to project anal-retentive vanity. When he showed up on the set, the director didn't say anything to John about how he looked. Figuring he was on the right track, he shot the first scene with his cheeks sucked in. Problem was, like most movies, the scenes were filmed out of order. And over the course of the three-week shoot, occasionally, an unexpected face cramp would make it impossible to affect the pinched look he had cooked up for his character. Some of the time he was able to maintain only one hollow cheek through an entire take, and sometimes would completely forget to make the face altogether.

John told me that he invited eight of his friends to the screening of *Scandalous John*. Every time his character came on-screen he looked like somebody else, which made his buddies whoop and holler and scream with laughter. (That's what friends are for.) However, despite his inauspicious big screen debut, John learned a valuable lesson: don't imbue your character with any physical traits you don't have the endurance to sustain throughout the project. Of course, for John, this lesson did not translate to "be more conservative with the physical characterizations." Instead, he consciously set about building up his stamina so he could create and sustain any character trait he chose to portray. However, in his early career, the lessons just kept on coming. Lessons like: read the entire script.

John once told me about another uneven performance

he gave in an episode of *Kojak. Who loves ya, baby?* He landed the part of a jewel thief named Kenny Soames, but due to some sort of production assistant snafu had not received the entire script before the shoot. He only had the scene he had been handed at the audition. When he got to the set the next day, he was told they were printing an entire script and would get it to him at lunch. In the meantime, they'd shoot the first scene that he had memorized for the audition. John said to himself, "Jewel thief, okay . . . thug," and decided to play the character as a dumb guy. (John always maintained that keeping your mouth a little open on camera instantly subtracts a couple dozen IQ points.) The first half of the day went swimmingly. John was confident that he had nailed his portrayal of the jewel-thieving lug. The assistant director called a wrap for lunch and John was handed a freshly printed entire script.

John never made it to lunch. He sat in his trailer reading and sweating. To his horror, he realized that the character he had been playing as an imbecile was actually written as a genius. A Rhodes scholar, in fact. John adjusted his performance for the rest of the episode. When the *Kojak* episode finally aired on television, viewing audiences were treated to Kenny Soames, the intellectually morphing jewel thief—a one-man bell curve.

Many years later in August 1997, we were spending the first night in our new house and John was flipping through the channels on our TV. Despite the fuzzy half-assed cable reception, he caught a glimpse of Kenny Soames, slack-jawed, in his jewel thief outfit (the requisite black knit cap and turtleneck). He called me into the room with a level of excitement usually associated with seeing oneself on TV for the *first* time. He had not seen it since it first aired in 1974. We rolled around on the floor laughing. It was, to the gesture, exactly as he had recounted for the previous twenty-three years. For an actor, no impression is as lasting as the humbling experience of being unimpressive.

John was undaunted by his early missteps. As were the casting directors. Even though he was doing theater at night and taking acting classes most days, he continued auditioning and booking TV work. You name it, he did an episode of it—much to the chagrin of his father.

The fact that Tex was a film actor, a recording artist, and the master of ceremonies at the Grand Ole Opry did nothing to ease his mind about having a son in show business. All the crazed physical comedy and, God forbid, experimental theater John was involved in during his college years had not done a thing to allay Tex's trepidation about a life in the spotlight for his younger son. The first play at USC he saw John do was Jean Genet's *The Balcony*. It was all about prostitutes, pimps, and the horrors of revolution. John said that his friend Jack Bender was sitting right behind his dad in the audience. Jack told him that Tex just got up in the middle of the show, like he was going to leave. He was pretty big by then and he pretty much dominated the ninety-nine-seat theater. He stood for a moment or two and then sat back down.

After the show, Jack went up to Tex and said, "Mr. Ritter, I just was wondering, is everything okay? I thought you were going to leave?" Tex answered, "No, son, I just had to stretch. That play never stopped." And then John's professor, the director of the play, went up to him and asked, "So Mr. Ritter did you like the play?" He replied, "Well, it certainly wasn't *Rebecca of Sunnybrook Farm*." Tex had a great sense of humor. John knew that his dad was not easy with the accolades or the compliments, but when you did get a compliment from him, you knew it came from the heart.

John told me that his dad was opposed to him being an actor because he didn't want him to be out of work all the time. He said Tex used to say, "Well, I got one son who is out there at USC studying to be an actor, which means I'll be singing 'The Boll Weevil' until I'm ninety-five, trying to get him some money."

Tex had a point. Luckily for John, it was at USC where he met a fledgling lawyer, Bob Myman, who would become his business partner and lifelong friend. John always knew that Bob, who went on to become a very well-respected entertainment attorney, protected him and advised him like he was part of the family. Together they were an unstoppable team.

In 1972, John was hired as a semiregular on *The Waltons* to play Reverend Fordwick, a character whom John never failed to refer to as "Reverend Foreskin." The quality of the show, its message, and John's truly touching portrayal of the earnest but struggling young preacher helped to win Tex over.

While visiting his folks in Nashville at Christmas in 1973, John saw the film *East of Eden* for the first time. The movie had been made many years earlier, but seeing it at this time in his life resonated with John in a major way. He was inspired and determined to really connect with his father, so he talked to his dad about it. He told him about the scene where James Dean tries to buy his father's love and his father rejects him. John said, "I just have to tell you—before one of us dies—I love you. And so I won't be like James Dean, I need to hear that from you." Tex put his hand on John's shoulder, looked away and said, "Oh, well, I love you, too, son." About three weeks later, at the age of sixty-eight, Tex Ritter died of what was reported as a heart attack. Whether it really was a heart attack is not known. The community of genetic researchers and surgeons now highly suspect that in truth, John's father had succumbed to an undiagnosed aortic dissection, just as John would, almost thirty years later.

The most important lesson John learned was not on a movie set or soundstage. It was in his own heart. He had followed his instinct to reach out and connect to his dad. It turned out to be his last opportunity to do so. He always stressed to me and to his kids the importance of making sure the people you love understand how much they mean to you. He lived his life that way. No matter where you were, emotionally or logistically, John made sure, every day, that you knew he loved you.

chapter 4

....

Daddy No Beard

John's three oldest kids, Jason, Carly, and Tyler Ritter were born during *Three's Company*'s eight-year run from 1977 to 1984. They grew up with the show and became pretty used to seeing their dad on television. However, when Stella was two and I tried to point John out to her on a Nick at Night rerun, she simply wasn't having it.

Aside from the first few weeks of Stella's life, John had worn a beard for as long as she had known him. I have movies of John leaning over a wide-eyed Baby Stella with her tiny feet pressed against his beard. He would interview her, asking questions and then rubbing the soles of her teeny little feet on his cheeks to elicit coos and gurgles that he would interpret as replies. Both fully engaged, the two of them would "dialogue" back and forth—for long stretches of time, without ever breaking eye contact. As an infant, she would see him enter the room and stretch out all four of her limbs toward him in preparation for another multisensory discussion. I have always maintained that these early "pieds-a-têtes" must have been the genesis of Stella's precocious conversational skills. The Daddy that the two-year-old Stella had always known was beefy, bearded, and three-dimensional. No wonder that when I pointed at the screen and insisted that the skinny, smooth-faced kid in the white bell-bottoms was her dad she thought I was nuts.

Her mom's delusion that this guy on the TV was Dad perplexed her, but Stella finally put the pieces of the puzzle together. Oddly, what made it all make sense for her was not his voice, the usual giveaway; it was seeing Jack Tripper walk straight into a door and being smashed in his face. The way his eyes crossed and his lips pursed before shaking it off and proceeding to walk smack into the door again was completely recognizable to her. John had been entertaining her from the moment she was born with his unique brand of physical comedy. *This*, she recognized. If the guy on television *wasn't* John, then clearly this Jack Tripper guy seemed to be stealing all of Dad's best bits.

From that day on, Stella referred to the character and the show as "Daddy No Beard." John got a huge kick watching Stella watch *Daddy No Beard*. Stella would always take his face in her hands and turn his head toward the TV, as if to say, "What are you looking at me for? You're missing it. This guy is good."

Growing up, to me *Three's Company* was that hilarious show that my parents insisted on watching with me every week when I was in high school. I really wanted my own TV so I could watch the jiggling and giggling and enjoy the double entendres alone. I thought John was adorable, but it made me wildly uncomfortable to know that my parents felt the same way. If my mom explained to me once, she explained it to me a thousand times: John was only *pretending* to be gay on the show. He was a straight actor, playing a straight character pretending to be *gay* in order to live with his two female roommates. I could tell she was having fun being in on the joke . . . and proud of herself for using the politically correct word "gay." I had to employ intense muscle control to stop my teenage eyes from rolling all the way out of my head.

The most painful aspect of watching *Three's Company* with my parents was clocking their looks back and forth to each other at every one of the show's signature sex jokes. Painful. I knew so much more than they thought I did. I had copies of *The Joy of Sex* and *Everything You Always Wanted to Know About Sex but Were Afraid to Ask* hidden in my room. My dad had a habit of loudly announcing random facts at what seemed to me to be the most risqué moments. I never fully understood his non sequitor outbursts until I found myself, all these years later, doing the same thing when watching TV with Stella. Occasionally, a seemingly family-friendly sitcom busts out with a racy joke or situation. Channeling my dad, I guess, I do my best to talk over it and divert her attention. Nowadays, that just sends Stella and me into a full on wrestling match for the remote control. Damn you, TiVo.

During the eight years of *Three's Company*, John worked with guest stars ranging from classically trained stage actors to fashion models. Each guest star would start off at their own speed, clumsy or confident; some of them really struggled and others showed up on day one having directed and plotted out the entire show in their heads. Guest star–wise, he maintained that everybody had something to bring to the party. According to him, even those most unfamiliar with the sitcom rhythm were able to catch up and bring their talents to bear for the studio audience.

The exception to the rule seemed to be stand-up comedians. He understood that for guys who were used to being on stage alone, ensembles would, naturally, not be their strong suit. For the most part, John accepted that they just had a very different way of working. It did, however, irk him when a certain propensity, vital to their competitive profession, spilled over to the sitcom set and beyond. The tendency to withhold laughter, pervasive among most solo comedians, drove him nuts. Nothing irked him more than a joke or bit being met with a deadpan utterance of "funny," as opposed to a genuine laugh. This did, however, make him even more appreciative of the truly magnanimous performers he knew. The few. The not-so-proud. Robin Williams, Richard Lewis, and Paul Reiser were among a handful of talents who genuinely played with him. For John, goofing around with these brilliant ego-free comics was nirvana.

I always suspected that his perception that all of the guest stars around him miraculously rose to the occasion had more to do with him than with them. A lot of actors are referred to as "generous" by their costars, and John embodied the trait like no one else. For someone who could have commanded the stage and held all of our rapt attention by himself, it was clear that he relished the relationship with his acting partners. Even though John had heard it hundreds and hundreds of times over the years, and we still hear about him today, I don't know whether he truly understood the powerful effect that he had on his fellow actors.

The confidence and playfulness and absolute joyfulness that John exuded made you feel like you could do no wrong. Being with John on set was a powerful experience. Powerful, not only for the comedic acting tips a more observant guest star might glean but for the greater life lesson of gratitude. John was grateful to be working and to have been given the opportunity to do what he did best. It was natural for him to "play" it forward every day. He exuded the spirit of comedy.

Many were the times that I was on a set with John in the nineties and a production assistant or a cameraman would call him Jack, not even knowing they had made a mistake. Not wanting to embarrass them by correcting their error, John would usually just answer to the name Jack and throw a knowing smile my way. I always picked up on the fact that most of the cast and crew he worked with in his post–*Three's Company* years had to try hard not to gush. When someone would get John alone at the craft service table or a group of guys would work up the nerve to ask him about specific episodes, no one could have been more gracious than John. A born storyteller like his dad Tex, John would hold court for a while. He would regale the cast and crew with stories that would leave them with tears of laughter in their eyes, much to the chagrin of more than a few second assistant directors. Wrangling everyone back to their posts after a session of impromptu John Ritter storytelling was not the easiest of tasks.

John, however, was able to change gears instantly and immediately throw himself back into whatever comedic or dramatic scene ensued. John's sense of fun combined with his total professionalism engendered an inspiring atmosphere of camaraderie. I've never seen any performer imbue a set with more energy of purpose. One of the very few times I ever saw John blush was when I shared this observation with him; I told him he was the only star quarterback who doubled as the head cheerleader.

The other scenario that played itself out regularly was that anytime we dined, anywhere in the world, the chef would invariably make his or her way out of the kitchen to meet John. So many times, these guys and gals would tell John that they became chefs because of him. His character's epic eight-year struggle to make a name for himself and run his own restaurant, Jack's Bistro, was very inspirational for this crowd. This was before the Food Network. At the time there were Julia Child, The Galloping Gourmet, and Jack Tripper.

Each chef wanted to know if John could actually whip together a gourmet meal. They were always incredulous when he would admit that he couldn't boil water. (Although, he was inordinately boastful of the fact that he could crack an egg with one hand.) They would actually argue with him about his cooking skills. "Oh come on, John (or Jack), I saw you make *crème de whatever* with my own eyes. It was brilliant." Television magic was what it was. John always said that the script supervisor would have to teach him the names of fancy French dishes phonetically.

Pronouncing the words correctly made him nervous and he would often screw it up.

Nothing deterred his chef-fans from their ardent appreciation of all things Jack Tripper. They would always bring out their signature dish for him, whether he ordered it or not, and hover anxiously while he tasted it. While he was still eating, they would ask for his honest opinion of their food, to which, pointing to his mouth, he would invariably reply, "This is not chewing—my teeth are applauding."

Chefs are not the only overly attentive fans of the show. Not unlike Trekkies, *Three's Company* fans are known for their diligent attention to detail. The facts ranging from the characters' middle names to the artwork on the apartment walls are chronicled and shared by observant devotees worldwide. Never was this phenomenon more evident than in March of 2001. At the time, Stella, John, and I were living in New York for his Broadway run in Neil Simon's *The Dinner Party*. As John loved to tell it: "We were just sitting there minding our own business . . ." when we got a very interesting phone call from John's fabulous longtime assistant, Susan Wilcox. Up to that point, she probably thought she had heard and seen it all. *The New York Observer* had called for a comment from John about the "episode 161 controversy." Apparently, one *on the ball* Nick at Night viewer got a little more than they bargained for when they slowed down the rerun of that episode, named "The Charming Stranger." When Jack plopped down on his bed in a T-shirt and blue boxers, they caught a glimpse of, as John put it, "one of the twins." Charming stranger indeed.

A viewer reported the risqué nanosecond to the network. (Freeze frame: not just for *Fatal Attraction* anymore.) A representative from Nickelodeon responded. He confirmed that, upon review, indeed, one of the Ritter family jewels had been unintentionally and momentarily exposed. He went on to reassure the public that the offending frames would be cut out of the episode for future airings.

When Susan called John asking for a comment for the *Observer* reporter, pronto, as they were about to go to press, John looked at me and said, "Amy?" I always work best under pressure and he knew it. I would like to thank the Mars candy company for my inspiration. The *Observer* article ran with John's quote: "I'm requesting that Nickelodeon air both versions, edited and unedited, because sometimes you feel like a nut, and sometimes you don't."

After it appeared in the paper, he used that line every time he was asked about the kerfuffle. He never failed to credit me. I know that joke was on his Top 10 List of The Best Things Amy Ever Gave Me, along with Stella . . . and eight other things I can't talk about.

chapter 5

If I Can Fake It There . . .

I visited New York for the second time during the summer of 1983, before my senior year of college. I had been in school for only three years, but after my father died, my heart really wasn't in it anymore. I was definitely going to school for him. I had—literally—given it the old college try. (My version of it, anyway.) By my junior year, I had enrolled in only theater and art classes and was a zillion credits away from graduating. I certainly was not on any kind of credible path to my bachelor-o-farts degree. So instead of moving back into the dorm in September, I packed my bags and moved to the Big Apple.

I ended up working as a hostess at O'Neal's on Forty-third Street and eventually started living there as well; 147 West 43rd Street was a very well-known address. The previous establishment had been Rosoff's, a restaurant and hotel that had stood at that site for sixty-three years. The hotel had been home to Fanny Brice of Ziegfeld Follies fame. For those of you scratching your heads—hello? Fanny Brice? The actual human being, on whose life story the Barbra Streisand play/movie *Funny Girl* was based. Still scratching your head? Rent it, *it's like buttuh.*

The hotel was all but abandoned by the time I moved in. There were only a couple of other tenants in the place, and, reportedly, a ghost or two. I was not concerned. I had plowed through my ghost/reincarnation/psychic phenomenon phase in high school. From ages fourteen through seventeen I willingly compartmentalized my Catholic belief system and my wild curiosity about all things paranormal. My parents would have freaked out if they had known how much I was reading on those taboo subjects. My sole outlet for discussion was my very cool, very open-minded brother Rex. Always ready to debate the possibility of everything and anything, he was a sounding board for me and my mystical musings.

Even though I didn't really buy the whole haunted hotel story, a couple of weeks into living there, I did have what would have passed as a paranormal encounter to a less cynical mind. I woke up in the middle of the night with the distinct feeling that someone or something was sitting on my bed. There was heaviness in the air. There was also a strange smell in the room. I just closed my eyes and pretended it wasn't happening (kind of a reoccurring theme in my life). I remember waking up in the next morning and chalking it up to the fact that I had eaten my first meal at an Indian restaurant the night before.

Living in Times Square in 1983, I had bigger worries than ghosts. This was back in the day before Times Square resembled downtown Disney. There were a lot of bad guys. And bad girls. *Beep, Beep, Heeey—Beep, Beep.* Before moving there, I had been living in Brooklyn on Atlantic Avenue between Hoyt and Bond. I took the train every day to and from Times Square, which was always an adventure. My subway stop was right by the *New York Times* building, and was at the time, reportedly, the most dangerous subway station in Manhattan. And by *dangerous* I don't mean there was the possibility of slipping on somebody's freshly hocked goober and frying on the third rail, although the likelihood of that was high. *The most dangerous subway station meant the most murders.* Perfect. From college in Detroit to this: next stop, hell.

There were a couple of months of nightly unaccompanied 1:00 a.m. commutes back home to Brooklyn, so I had my share of close calls. One harrowing near-mugging stands out. I faked out the bad guys by jumping out of the train at the last possible moment as the doors were closing at a totally unfamiliar stop. Not the best move. I had my purse but not my bearings. After sitting on an empty subway platform for an hour, attempting to lower my heart rate from hummingbird back to human, I warily boarded another train. I was a nervous wreck. I was convinced that the little *Mission Improbable* scenario that I had just lived through was probably the last of my luck. I didn't want to tempt fate. I weighed my options (none) and decided to take my chances aboveground and move to Times Square.

During that time I was a nonworking actress. Let me help with the pronunciation: the "nonworking" is silent, and "actress" is pronounced "hostess." But I was happy just to be living in Manhattan, absorbing and being absorbed by the big city. The theatergoing public would fill the restaurant to the rafters from about six to seven-thirty, pissing and moaning about their tables and their reservations until they had "waited at the bar" long enough for an attitude-adjusting refreshment or two. The crowd would die down between eight and ten. Then a little after ten o'clock, the public and a handful of performers would start to trickle back in for more drinking or eating, but not a whole hell of a lot of tipping. Not for the hostess anyway. I think you pretty much have to be designated as the maître d' to get that kind of acknowledgment. Tommy Tune and Twiggy (they were doing *The Boyfriend* at the time) were the exception. They always handed me a little something. All through the fall it was the same routine: just feeding people and keeping them happy and tipsy and sending them off in time to see Broadway shows.

As December rolled around, I started to get calls from back home. Not the good kind. Things in Cincinnati were getting tricky. My mom was not doing well. It had been a year and a half since my father died, and my mom was pretty much giving up. Then the bipolar disorder she had been wrestling with for years once again swept her up into a physically debilitating manic episode. This time, Mom was so frail and broken that we all knew she might not live through it. She didn't. We lost her on January 31, 1984.

When I came back to New York after the funeral, my fellow restaurant workers were very supportive. They gave me a homemade oversize card that they had all signed, yearbook style, with sympathy shout-outs. Busboys, chefs, waitresses, managers, and maintenance workers poured out their hearts in English and in Spanish. Everybody did their best in an awkward situation, welcoming their coworker back from burying her mother. Far and away the best came from a bartender who later went on to become a pretty successful writer in Hollywood. He scribbled a simple but profound "Chin up, Slick!"—words that were perhaps more appropriate to say to a buddy who has accidentally dented your freshly repainted Camero, but it's the one message I remember.

All of us semisquatters got kicked out of the hotel in May of that year. I moved to a run-down loft situated across from Madison Square Garden on Thirty-fourth Street. It was neither intended nor zoned to be a living space. It was there that I encountered the biggest cockroach of my life (outside of show business). Volkswagen size. At some point I just had to say to myself, "Okay, apparently I am going to coexist with this creature. I'm in his world, this is my roommate." Oh, and there were mice—not just a couple, a community. When the weather began to really warm up, a much more insidious evil began to creep—make that *waft*—up to the fourth-floor window. The revolving door on the corner of Macy's spun around all day long, belching Obsession and Poison from the bowels of the perfume department onto the street. Nothing says "midtown" like the cloying scent of overmarketed perfume mingled with urine and garbage.

By summer, I was employed by another O'Neal's establishment, O'Neal's Balloon, on Sixty-first Street (so named because at the time the use of the word "saloon" was forbidden due to an outdated Prohibition-era law). It was directly across from Lincoln Center for the Performing Arts, a complex that houses the Lincoln Center Theater, New York City Ballet, New York City Opera, Metropolitan Opera, and New

York Philharmonic. It also includes the School of American Ballet and The Juilliard School. So there I was, AWOL from college, surrounded by the real deal.

At this location, there seemed to be a bit of a class system. The pecking order was set. But hierarchy is a concept I always seem to be able to sidestep by pretending I don't notice it. The waiters and waitresses for the most part were cool, but very cliquey. I always told myself that I never became a waitress because I was a vegetarian and had a bad relationship with burgers and things and didn't want to be around food that much. Truth is: I probably could not have done the math on the bills. I was just there to show the folks to their table, take reservations, and occasionally field grievances. I'd rather have been the one the customers complained to than the one they complained about. I also got to kibitz with the regulars at the bar, *Cheers* style.

It was very exciting working there because I got to have lots of one-on-one conversations with artists who performed at Lincoln Center. Mikhail Baryshnikov was the artistic director of the American Ballet Theater and would walk across the street every so often to the Balloon. He would perch at the bar and have a beer with his baseball cap down over his eyes. When I would get up the nerve to talk to him, he would entertain me with a story or two about anything but ballet. He was always a gentleman, and always distracting. His preferred bar stool was positioned in such a way that a conversation with him required me to stand with my back to the door. It's surprising how many angry tourists can stack up like planes over LaGuardia on a foggy day when you are engaged in small talk with one of the most famous dancers in the world. Another of the world's most famous dancers at the time also occasionally frequented the Balloon. He never spoke to me—I guess I wasn't *Godunov* for him.

I was working every day at the edge of the cultural center of New York City. Every day I was with entertainers from the world of theater, television, opera, and dance. I was happy to be a spectator at that point. I had done some play readings and gone out on a couple of auditions, but I never told anyone at work that I was an actress. I was very happy to be a mere hostess in their eyes. It seemed that everyone I worked with was a performer and they were all constantly sweating it and bitching about their auditions. There was a palpable amount of negativity in the air. I just never threw in. I was busy just honing my human-being skills, being a good citizen and holding down a job. I had lost both my parents in the previous year and a half. It was all kind of hitting me at once.

In December 1984, the Balloon staff was all atwitter about the fact that J. Michael Bloom, an agent in New York, London, and L.A. was going to be at a party that the O'Neal brothers were throwing. I went over to pour coffee at Michael's table, and when he started to talk to me, I ignored him. He had a little bit of arrogance about him and, of course, everybody was in "Hi, I'm Jennifer, I'll be your actress—uh, waitress!" mode, bending over backward and doing their act. So when I went up to his table, he tried to talk to me and I talked to whomever he would have considered the lowliest person at the table. I can't remember, or maybe decorum does not permit me to say, who that was. He kept trying to talk to me and I kept putting him off, saying, "Excuse me, I'm speaking. Hold on. Take turns." I was being sassy and making jokes with this other person. I think my attitude piqued his interest. Then he kind of said some version of "Do you know who I am?" and I said, "Who doesn't?" He asked if I was an actress and I said, "Who isn't?" So he asked me to come to his office and audition for him. Of course, I was jumping up and down inside but played it very cool.

This is how it goes: You audition for agents, hoping that one will take you on and want to represent you. Their job is to send you out to casting directors on—what else?—more auditions, in the hopes of being called back to audition for the director. And so it goes, forever. Very, very few people escape this cycle of auditioning. So I went in and auditioned for him with a couple of monologues I had done in school. I have no idea what I did or how I did it, but he took me on as a client and told me that he wanted me to come to L.A. for pilot season. And just like that I was piloted in a big old jet airliner that did carry me too far away (Steve Miller Band . . . anyone?) to Los Angeles. I never did tell the waiters and waitresses and bartenders at the Balloon. But I told Jimmy, the manager, and he was kind enough to say he would hold my job for a couple months. In case Hollywood sent me packing, he would let me slip back into my hostessing job.

When I was settled in L.A., the agency sent me to a meeting at Lorimar, which is no longer around, but, lordy, they were big in the day. They were doing *Dallas, The Waltons, Knot's Landing,* and a load of other 1980s hits. I had just hit town a few weeks earlier equipped with a set of hot rollers, one pair of heels (white lace-top anklets optional), and two audition dresses with shoulder pads. We're talking 1985 here. I can't even remember the name of the TV pilot

I was trying out for, but after reading for the part along with a gaggle of other hot-rollered, big-shouldered twentysome-things, I gathered up my things to go. I couldn't help but notice a steady stream of decidedly more sophisticated and exotic actresses signing in to read for a different casting di-rector. I snuck a peak at the sheet. "Rockhopper." So I put my name on that list and picked up the sides (the script ex-cerpts) of which I could make neither heads nor tails.

When the casting assistant called my name from the list, I fluffed my hair, threw back my shoulders, and walked into the unknown. I very well could have been tossed out on my rear. I played dumb, as if I had accidentally put my name on the wrong sign-in sheet. The casting director was on to me immediately, but she let me read anyway. She explained that the part everyone was reading for was that of a Russian spy. Again . . . 1985. She asked me if I needed time to prepare. I told her that I was ready. Such is the bravery of youth. I pro-ceeded to pull a Russian accent out of my . . . let's say "rep-ertoire." By that I mean, I re-created the accent from my highly acclaimed turn as Olga in Chekhov's *Three Sisters* . . . hold on . . . my mistake, that's not my life. I actually lifted the Russian accent from archvillain Natasha on the Bull-winkle cartoons. Surprisingly, the casting lady liked it. I got called back half a dozen times and finally ended up at CBS in front of a roomful of executives. Yikes.

When I found out that I had booked the pilot and would be playing the part of Sonya Petrova, the first thing I did was call home. And call home. And call home. I was twenty-three. This was my first job in show business, and I was pretty psyched. This was way, way, way before e-mail. I made twenty or so calls that day, one to each person in my ever-expanding family. I not only had to tell them about my job but I also had to explain the premise of the show, the audition process, and what pilot season was. Cut to a year later: my relatives asking me if I was "getting points on the backend" and if I was going to ask for a "single-card billing in the credits"— fast learners, those Yasbecks. The pilot was going to shoot in New York and I could not have been more excited.

Parker Stevenson starred as the American spy, along with Pat Carroll (an absolute doll, I loved her), and Janis Paige, who was nice enough. It was a very old-school cast. The most exciting part for me was that Bill Bixby—*The Courtship of Eddie's Father, The Incredible Hulk*—was going to direct the pilot. I had left New York for my adventure in Los Angeles only a few weeks before. Now I was back, but this time with wardrobe and hair.

The first half of the first day of filming was spent cooling my heels on the set and trying to get a sense of how the whole thing was put together. I watched the other actors film their scenes, but I mostly focused my attention on the assistant director. He was speaking a language to the cast and crew that I needed to learn . . . fast:

"Last looks": This is everyone's last chance to look at the actors and the set and figure out what needs to be done before the camera rolls.

"Final touches": We're about to roll the camera. Hair, Makeup, Wardrobe—do what needs to be done to make these actors presentable. Get in there and tweak those bad boys.

I listened closely and prepared for my close-up. The very first scene I ever filmed—much like the pilot's chances of being picked up—was a long shot. I was an overly coiffed Russian spy in a red leather jacket, striding purposefully down Fifth Avenue toward the Plaza Hotel. We filmed take after take of Sonya Petrova clomping her way from point A to point B. When the director had gotten the take he was looking for, he yelled, "Cut!" and then signaled the assistant director, who called, "Moving on!"

"Moving on": We're going on to the next scene, like it or not.

The first day of shooting, Bill asked for a restaurant recommendation to take me and Parker to lunch. Oh, yes indeed, I suggested O'Neal's Balloon. As far as most of the staff knew, I was just on sabbatical somewhere. The idea of walking back into that restaurant with a job—much less with The Hulk and a Hardy Boy—was beyond satisfying.

When I was working there, everyone would make a big fuss when ex-waiter Ed O'Neill (no relation to the boss) would stop by to visit his then fiancée, Catherine Russoff. No less awe-inspiring than glimpsing the Loch Ness monster or Bigfoot, being in the presence of an honest-to-God *working actor* (the rarest of species) would temporarily short circuit the place. All but ignoring the tipping public, we would hover around his booth clutching sweaty glasses of Tab and baskets of sourdough rolls that would just have to remain undelivered for the time being. Besides being one of the only people we knew who was making a living at doing theater and films, Ed was also a genuinely gracious guy. His stories thrilled and inspired us. Who knew, at the time, that by way of the circuitous route that winds its way through showbiz and real life, we would eventually be connected?

In 1986, Ed was cast in *Married with Children*. He starred, of course, as Al Bundy the beloved-ish husband of Peg Bundy, played by Katey Sagal. Many years later, Katey would go on to star in *Eight Simple Rules,* playing Kate Hennessy, the wife of Paul Hennessy, who was played by my real-life husband, John.

John always loved the notion that everyone in the world is connected by no more than six degrees of separation. It validated the feeling he had always had of how close we all really are. After he died, I began to realize that his fans felt zero degrees of separation from him. To them he was a part of their lives. They had grown up with him. They had lost one of their own.

I remember the first time John and I went to New York together. He asked me to show him where exactly I shot that first scene in *Rockhopper*. We walked that long block alongside the park and I told him how I had felt like a visitor in the show business world that day; listening so intently, trying to interpret what was to be my new language. It's always a struggle when you find yourself in a new role, both on the set and off. When I'm in New York now and I find myself on that stretch of sidewalk, I still hear the assistant director calling out his commands. But through the prism of my life now, the words have taken on yet another layer of meaning for me.

Last looks.

Final touches.

Moving on.

chapter 6

Icon Tact

Whenever John was asked for his take on celebrity, he always said that being famous is like being out in the sun. It feels really good and warm. You can bask in it, drink it in, and appreciate it. But if you stay out in it too long, you get completely burned and have to find shade. He insisted that nobody in their right mind, except for maybe Zsa Zsa Gabor, would actually want to be famous every day and every night. For John, this was never more apparent than in the men's room. More than once, a fan making his way from the stall to the sink would stop at the urinal and want to shake "Jack Tripper's" otherwise engaged hand. That alone was reason enough to prove his point that sometimes celebrity just isn't all it's cracked up to be. But John's love-hate relationship with fame really started years before he found success as an actor.

When he and Tommy were little boys out with their dad for the day, they would, without fail, be stopped several times by fans wanting their moment, their one moment, with Tex. In those days, very few people carried cameras around with them, seeing as most cameras were the size of a toaster. But autographs? Autographs were something everyone could try to get. And everyone wanted Tex Ritter's autograph. He was larger than life.

John and Tommy were just like any other kids out with their dad, except for the fact that they'd be stopped every ten feet by what John would come to refer to for the rest of his life as "fan mines." Whenever they hit one, John would often implore his father to keep moving, saying, "Dad, come on let's go. Why can't we go?" And Tex would say, "Boys, these are the people who buy your daddy's albums. And you know what happens when they do that? I earn a living. I make money, and then we can pay for whatever we do, like go to the store or out to dinner, you know? These people are good people."

Tex made sure that his boys understood at a young age that performers and their performances do not exist in a vacuum. Not unlike the proverbial tree that falls in the forest question: If a cowboy sings on a stage, and no one is there to hear him . . . can he make a living? John and Tommy got it, and they accepted the reality that sharing Tex with his fans was part of the deal. It happened so much that they would entertain themselves by watching people's expressions as they screwed up the courage to approach their dad. John said it was always fascinating to see how the fans reacted to finally having the chance at an audience with their cowboy idol. No matter how many times it happened, the surrealism of the moment was never lost on the boys. They saw "Dad," while everyone else saw "movie star."

Even though autograph hounds and Tex Ritter fans were a nuisance to him as a little boy, John would end up signing tens of thousands of autographs in his life. But he did it on his own terms. Having grown up navigating a sea of fan mines, he vowed early on that if he ever became famous, he would make sure that his family felt more important than the fans. And as his kids can attest, he kept that promise.

John always said that he would prefer to shake hands with someone, look them in the eye, and have some genuine human connection, rather than just write his name on a piece of paper or a photograph. Many were the times that he would very sweetly shake hands with an autograph seeker and tell them, "I'm just a dad today. It was very nice meeting you." John's feeling was that if you're truly nice to people, sincerely nice, 95 percent of the people will respect the fact that you're with your family. They will be cool with you if you are genuine with them.

This technique was never more "in play" than when he was at Dodger Stadium. John was the most genuine baseball fan I have ever met. America's *pastime* was John Ritter's *bliss-time*. He used baseball analogies in his everyday life, as we all do to some extent—but my favorite was his version of Lennon's "life is what happens when you're making other plans." When searching for a way to express the unpredictability of show business or politics, even day-to-day life, John would say, "Anything can happen in baseball." When he was in the stands during a game, he tried never to sign an autograph. It baffled him that somebody would take time away from root-root-rooting for the home team to come over and ask him to sign their scorecard. He really just wanted to be a fan with a mitt (because you never know when you'll be called to greatness) and a bag of peanuts.

Every so often he'd see a little kid making a beeline down to his row with a Sharpie and a mission. He would always walk the little guy back up to the top of the aisle, keeping one eye on the game, and hastily sign the autograph. He would pat the little tyke on the head then lope back down to his seat and ask us, "Wud I miss?!"

When Tyler was thirteen, John invited him along to play in a charity baseball game at his alma mater, USC. I was thrilled to be tagging along. Tyler not only shared his dad's love of the game but had also been coached by him into being an amazing player.

It was shaping up to be the perfect day, but anything can happen in baseball. The weather refused to play fair and the game was rained out. We all ended up huddled under a huge tent trying to stay dry. Fans lined up and clamored for John's autograph. They had all brought their cameras to the game and were not leaving (who could blame them?) without a picture or two. John obliged, good-naturedly, and stood in one spot for almost an hour, kibitzing with the folks, signing all manner of sports equipment and programs and T-shirts and baseball caps. He put his arm around everyone and their brother for a photo, dipped a few grandmas in romantic embraces for the cameras, and basically saved the day.

For John, this kind of thing was like falling off a log: easy for him, yet truly exciting for everyone that got a chance to have their John Ritter moment. It came naturally to him and he fed on the energy of the crowd. I had seen him in this mode hundreds of times. Tyler had not. Watching his dad work the crowd—make that *play with the crowd*—made his face light up with an astonished grin. The sheer number of fans who clamored for John's attention, and the indefatigable energy that his father seemed to possess, fascinated Tyler. All the way back to the car, he peppered John with questions: "Dad, how many autographs do you think you just signed back there? How many do you think you signed, like, in your life? A thousand? Or thousands and thousands? Like ten thousand? A million?"

John finally said, "Ty, why do you need to know a number?"

Tyler replied, "Just trying to figure out how much of this you can do."

John was touched. He was a very humble man who never felt the need to pat himself on the back. But that night he admitted to me that he felt proud of himself. The fact that the day's marathon fan-fest seemed a novel occurrence to his son meant that he had done something right. He had kept the promise he made to himself as a kid that his family would always know that they came first.

To keep the fan mines to a minimum, John always wore sunglasses and one of his many caps in public. Venturing out into the world au natural was a surefire way to get recognized in ten seconds flat. The vastness of his hat collection was a necessity and yet there were limits. I would beg him not to go out in one of what I lovingly referred to as his "Von Dutch toaster cozies," the '90s trucker-style hats are square and spongy and unflattering on everybody—except for Queen Latifah. They always put me in the mind of Choo-Choo Charlie, the Good & Plenty train engineer from old commercials.

The few times that John did try to change up his tried and true disguise it did not go well. Once we threw caution to the wind when he decided to stroll through midtown Manhattan without the usual cap and glasses routine. Instead, he opted for a custom-made set of gnarly yellow dentures and a funny walk. Half a block into this grand experiment, we passed two teenage girls who did a double take and screamed. By their reaction, he was less than incognito and more like incog . . . *"Neato! It's John Ritter— Oh man, in person, his teeth are sooo messed up!"*

John's baseball caps were more than a prop or wardrobe; they became part of him. When he couldn't bear to watch his beloved Dodgers in a tight spot, or he found a scene in a horror movie a tad too gruesome, he would turn his cap around and look through the tiny air holes in the back. He said it was like looking through pinholes in his eyelids. He wanted to close his eyes, but he didn't want to miss anything. It just seemed safer in there for him.

John had the same reaction watching fellow actors on talk shows. If the interview started to go south, he would curl up into a ball or pace the room, if he wasn't already peering through the eyelid pinholes of a baseball cap. He couldn't turn off the television, but he also couldn't quite bear to watch. It killed him to see actors die a thousand deaths on talk shows—especially when they were completely unaware that they were solidifying the public's opinion that performers are arrogant a-holes.

Even with all of his improvisational skills and off-the-cuff charm, John's least favorite character to play was John Ritter. He preferred working from a script. Surprisingly, this fact kept him from doing what everyone thought would have been his show. John always loved *Saturday Night Live;* he absolutely loved it. He loved every cast member of every season, knew all of the show's signature characters, and always used *SNL* lingo around the house. John was asked to host a couple of times, but he just couldn't bring himself to do it. Whenever he watched the monologues at the opening of the show, he would start to sweat. That was the part that spooked him. That was the only reason he didn't do the show—tanking live was one thing, but tanking live while just being himself was absolutely out of the question. He shuddered at the idea of it.

Despite declining the invitations to do *SNL,* John accepted just about everything that came his way. Most actors sift through requests, only responding to high-profile commencement ceremonies (although he definitely did speak at his share of those) and invitations to appear on *Inside the Actors Studio* (that guy loved John and would have had him on anytime . . . I'm just saying). For John, however, wherever students or fledgling actors of any stripe were, he would show up at the drop of a fax. Much to the chagrin of his agents and publicists, John felt compelled to go where he was called. He lent himself freely to any public or private venue where he could use the draw of his celebrity to raise money for or lift the spirits of young performers.

John always paid for his theater seats, despite the protests of producers, directors, and box office managers who insisted that his tickets should be complimentary. He was always more than happy to support theater. Whenever he attended high school, community, or local theater, word would travel backstage that he was in the audience. And at the end of the show, he would always go back and meet the cast. Nobody could make you feel better about yourself and your performance than John could. The secret to his compliments was their laser-sharp specificity. Somehow he could watch what you were doing onstage from inside of you. Maybe it had less to do with remote vision than it did with the fact that he knew every trick in your bag. He probably invented most of them. Somehow John would catch the moment that each performer was most proud of and be able to specifically and honestly react to their intentions.

As much as we were John's audience—a fascinated, grateful, thoroughly entertained audience of millions, grateful to observe him, happy to be entertained, fascinated by him—he was *our* audience . . . at the theater, in public, and at home. He was an observer, recording and decoding our every move, every smile, every grimace, every wince, and celebrating the qualities that make humans human.

John's warmth as a person made him seem familiar to fans in a way that extended beyond his iconic television persona. Every so often, someone would approach him, insisting that their husband, brother, or in the later years, father looked exactly like him. Exactly. As in "Oh my God it's freaky! You're not going to believe this. Hold on, I've got his picture in my wallet . . . see? He looks exactly like you, right?!" John would invariably search the fan's face for any trace of irony, shoot me a withering smile, and then pipe up with a convincing, "Wow! You weren't kidding. It's like looking in a mirror."

More often than not, John was not only confused but mildly insulted. He was anything but vain, but a few of those pictures were enough to shake even the most secure guy. Not only were most of the comparisons a stretch of the imagination, some were downright hilarious. He would always joke that *just once* he would like a fan to open their wallet and point to a picture of a handsome guy.

There were also the oh-so-awkward moments that would slowly tick by, after a hulking restaurant patron would lean in a little too close to deliver the "my wife just looooves you" line. Even after dozens of years of finding himself looking into the spiraling eyes of an anywhere from mildly buzzed to stinking drunk husband, who had apparently endured a marriage-long comparison to Jack Tripper, John was never quite sure where they were going with that opening line. Clearly, a good percentage of these guys were tanked up and ready for confrontation.

Luckily, John's default setting was programmed sometime in the early 1950s. John's mother, Dorothy, had always told her boys, "When you are speaking in public or in any new situation, you must think *everyone in this room loves me and I love everyone in this room.*" I was always amazed by how many of these guys were charmed by his smile and his hale-and-hearty handshake. John always behaved as if the big galoot was complimenting him, as opposed to firing the first shot over the bow. Apparently, this was enough to confuse and disarm most inebriated hooligans.

John knew that his fame was nothing to be scoffed at or thought of as a burden. Anyone on their sixteenth-plus minute knows how fickle the public is and how fleeting their affections can be. As much as he enjoyed the perks that came with fame, he was wise enough to know that it came with a serious responsibility. Nothing gave the career he had chosen more meaning than being able to use his celebrity for good, so he always happily complied with charitable requests. Most notably was his absolute devotion to United Cerebral Palsy.

When John's brother was diagnosed with cerebral palsy as a child, their mother, Dorothy, became an activist. Harnessing her unflagging optimism and legendary spirit, she joined with other parents to educate the public about this disease and to campaign for equal treatment and access under the law. In the 1970s, John gladly used the star power he had gained on television to host a national United Cerebral Palsy telethon for more than fifteen years. Enlisting his family and friends, John raised millions of dollars for the cause.

For John, the inevitable hassles that came along with celebrity were vastly outweighed by the opportunity that fame afforded him to make a difference in people's lives.

chapter 7

....

Like Sands Through the Hourglass

With my first paid acting job under my belt, and as fate would have it, under the radar, I was on my way to bigger and better things. Well, bigger things. Okay . . . things.

I had the opportunity to audition for *New Love, American Style*. The original *Love, American Style* was on from 1969 to 1974 and was pretty racy compared to most of the other prime-time fare. As a kid, I would watch the show, transfixed. I would fall asleep at night, straining to remember every detail. I knew the secret to being a grown-up was contained in that double entendre–laden hour of comedy. I just had to decode it.

I just knew there was a lot of hidden meaning in those sassy interstitial bits. In between the fifteen-minute story segments, before and after the commercials, they would show rolling brass beds being pushed down city streets by sexy, overteased, and ever-teasing nonspeaking actors. In our

1986 version of the show, there was a six-member comedy troupe of sorts slinging the corniest jokes you can imagine. If vaudeville is dead, then this was its groaning zombie. Our little troupe included the undisputed king of malapropisms, Norm Crosby, and one of my favorite actresses ever, Marcia Wallace. (I had always marveled at her droll delivery and killer timing as the secretary on *The Bob Newhart Show*.) And thanks to the amazing cast and crew, I had an absolute blast on the show.

It has always been and will always be the people with whom I get to work who make my job compelling. I know I'm supposed to love acting because I have a burning desire to tell a story. Not so much. People are my amusement, my amazement, my education. And having the opportunity to work with great actors and directors is one of the most thrilling aspects of the job.

In the spring of 1986, I landed a role on *Days of Our Lives*—or as I would come to think of it, *Four Months of My Life*. When I called my sister to tell her my good news it kind of blew her mind. The reason, as she tells it, is her remarkably historic and steadfast relationship with the show. When she brought her baby boy home from the hospital in 1965, she couldn't get him to take his afternoon bottle. Her doctor suspected that Ann could not sit still long enough for either of them to relax. Not the layabout type, she was a bit irked when he suggested she try watching television while she fed her little Bobby. The next day, she turned on the TV set and sat down in her rocking chair with Bobby on her lap. The first thing she saw was the iconic hourglass and the swelling strains of violin strings. As the voiceover was saying, "Like sands through the hourglass, so are the days of our lives," she realized she was about to see the very first episode of the new NBC soap opera. She settled in and never budged until her little sister was on the show twenty-one years later. Or something like that.

Soap operas are boot camp for actors. You have to learn lines more than fast, you get about one and a half takes to get them right, and in my case, very little to go on in terms of character analysis. "Like shit through a goose, so are the days of our lives . . ." Roman just opened the door one day, and lying there in the snow with a sprained ankle, was a helpless Olivia Reed. (I know, *Oliver Reed*—it was like I was the only one who noticed the similarity. I stopped bringing it up because everybody looked at me like I was crazy.) I was also never quite informed as to whether I was a good guy or a bad guy. Once, confused about my character's motivation in a scene, I asked, "Now, am I lying or am I telling the truth?" I was directed to "play it down the middle." Even though that suggestion seemed like a slap in the face to all those who had painstakingly imparted their wisdom to me at the University of Detroit Theater Program, I was unfazed. No storming off the set declaring, "I can't work like this!" for me. The operative word there is "work." So grateful was I to have a job on television that I would have "played it down the middle" forever.

Oh, but that was not to be. I knew my days on *Days* were numbered when I read in my script that Olivia was indeed a bad guy. She was the sister of the woman whom Roman accidentally killed, a woman who was married to the devilishly handsome Orpheus, who was holding Roman's wife Marlena hostage on an island and further tormenting Roman by placing me in his path, so he would fall in love with me and . . . I still don't know. All I know is, I laughed until I cried my false eyelashes off every day that I worked with George DelHoyo, who played my evil brother-in-law, Orpheus. I found George to be one of the most entertaining people I had ever met. At the drop of a hat, he would break out his dead-on impersonation of *SCTV*'s Dave Thomas impersonating Bob Hope. This tickled me to no end. It made the day fly by.

During my illustrious four-month run on *Days of Our Lives,* try as I might, I could never make myself cry. All kinds of sad and confusing, tear-worthy things were happening to Olivia Reed. Either she was one tough cookie, or the twenty-three-year-old actress portraying her had no idea how to cry on cue. Often I would employ The Method. Not the Stanislavsky Method, but The *Holy crap, a human being would be crying right now if this stuff was actually happening to her . . . I know! I'll stare directly into the overhead lights without blinking until the scene starts* Method.

And in fact, my technique did produce a kind of semicry— not quite crying exactly, but definitely a kind of *misty* effect—mostly on my vision for several hours afterward. On more than one occasion, the migraine headaches that I would invariably induce caused me to burst into dramatic, streaming, soap-opera sobs in the car on the way back to my apartment in Venice Beach—too late. My character was written out after four months by way of a devastating, unrequited confession of love (nope, no tears yet, dry as a bone), followed by a gunshot to the upper arm (which Olivia seemed to take surprisingly well).

John, on the other hand, was an amazing on-screen crier. The trick he used was a little something I never quite perfected, called . . . wait, I'm not sure how to pronounce it . . . *acting*—that's it. I still find it hard to watch anything he does where he gets teary because it tears me up. He really used his memory and his imagination to conjure up the physical expression he needed for the scene. There was a method to his sadness.

One of John's favorite acting stories was from his days on *The Waltons*. John loved absolutely everybody on that show. And in keeping with the gifted and grateful actor that he was, he would brighten everyone's day with humor and hijinks, while keeping the show going at the desired pace by being a professional when the camera was rolling. In his role as Reverend Fordwick, there was one scene where he had to preside over a church ceremony honoring Mom and Dad Walton on their anniversary. He had to deliver a lengthy, emotional monologue from the pulpit, while staring into the faces of his fellow actors, with whom he had been joshing around all day and all year. He got the giggles and could not pull himself together. And John-Boy was no help; Richard Thomas made him laugh the hardest. John struggled through the scene practically wetting his pants he was trying so hard not to laugh. At the same time, he was worried that he wasn't doing his job by giving Reverend Fordwick the gravitas called for in the scene.

When it was time for John-Boy to give his own monologue from the pulpit, John was praying that his friend Richard could get through the scene without breaking up, while secretly hoping that Richard would lose it, so he wouldn't be the only one making the cast and crew wait for him to pull himself together. To his surprise and amazement, Richard delivered his touching monologue flawlessly. He cried beautiful, slow tears and choked up just enough to see the flood of emotion right below the surface. After the "cut," there was a silence and then a rumble of quiet applause.

John said to Richard, "How the hell did you do that?" Richard then demonstrated that he had kept his hand in his front pocket during the scene, and had been pinching the edge of his scrotum hard enough to make himself cry. Ah . . . the magic of showbiz. This may explain why I never cried on *Days of Our Lives*. Olivia had chutzpah, but no balls.

After my short but memorable stint at soap opera boot camp, I was cast in a teeny-tiny role on *Dallas*. Appearing on this iconic show was absolutely mind-boggling to me at the time. In 1987, even though I didn't watch the show, I knew that everything was *Dallas* and *Dallas* was everything. My character Mary Elizabeth (no last name) was the skiing buddy of Jamie Ewing Barnes (two last names). Apparently, Jamie had been killed in an avalanche and I was the last person to see her alive. For my big debut on the show, I sported a cumbersome thigh-to-ankle cast. I hobbled over to the door to let in Cliff Barnes (Ken Kercheval), so I could tell him that his wife Jamie Ewing Barnes was dead.

By the way, Jamie was played by Jenny Lee Harrison (two first names) who had played Cindy Snow on *Three's Company*, the role of Chrissy's sister, who was added to the show during Suzanne Somer's contract dispute. I didn't work with her on *Dallas*, what with the whole "being killed by an avalanche" and all. But I did meet her in 2000, when Don Knotts received his star on the Hollywood Walk of Fame. I introduced myself to her as Mary Elizabeth, and told her I was happy she had dug her way out of the snow.

The overlapping and minimal degrees of separation in our business are as predictable and as borderline inbred as the British monarchy. If you work long enough in show-biz, you will end up running into the same people in different roles. Often, it takes a minute to remember what show you worked with them on and if they played your father, brother, husband—or they might have been a production assistant. Not unlike reincarnation, occasionally you will recognize someone from a former lifetime, but it's hazy. The same basic rules of karma apply: Do your job and try not to piss anybody off, because you never know where they will pop up down the line.

In 1987, I was finally able to realize my impossible childhood dream to be a mermaid. It started when I was seven years old. My sister Patti took me to see the re-release of Disney's *Peter Pan* at the Kenwood movie theater. All I could think, talk, and dream about afterward was the Neverland mermaids. *Flying? Who cares about flying?* I was transfixed by those saucy little nymphs. While partial nudity on its own does tend to stand out in a Disney cartoon, the addition of mysteriously affixed starfish pasties ratcheted up my interest level in a whole new way. I was growing up in a very clothed-minded family and I intended to get a peek—somewhere, somehow.

That summer my parents took me to Florida to visit Cape Canaveral, which had been renamed Cape Kennedy. I had been pestering them to visit NASA, and on the improbable chance that they may have had a future rocket scientist on their hands, they included a stop on our summer vacation itinerary. Little did they know that my request had nothing to do with the space program and everything to do with Barbara Eden. At the time, I was also more than a little obsessed with *I Dream of Jeannie*. After mermaids, scantily clad genies came in a close second. Even the network-approved, high-waisted, mom-jeans version of harem pants that Jeannie was required to wear did not faze me. Belly buttons were not necessary to pique my interest.

On the way to Florida, we stopped at Weeki Wachee Springs, home of the live mermaid show. Intellectually, I knew those girls were being zipped into their fins before appearing in the tank, and my dad explained that he suspected they were taking surreptitious hits from an oxygen tube as they intermittently ducked behind faux coral outcroppings. However, I wholeheartedly suspended my disbelief, knowing that only in doing so would I be able to fully enjoy the mermaid experience.

Twenty-ish years later, I set my sights on the role of Madison the Mermaid in the upcoming Disney Sunday Night Movie *Splash, Too*. It was a television sequel to the big-screen blockbuster *Splash*, which starred Tom Hanks and Daryl Hannah, and had been Disney Studios' initial foray into the realm of PG movies and beyond. *Splash*, produced under the new Touchstone banner, was a departure from the expected Disney fare on which they had made their reputation and vast fortune. The studio decided to produce a television movie that would serve as a "backdoor" pilot for a weekly series.

And being that I was then, and remain to this day, about a foot and a half shorter than Daryl Hannah, a new mermaid tail had to be made to my measurements. It was quite a beautiful creation: orange and gold and molded to my body for the kind of tailored fit you want in a mermaid tail. It was very heavy and confining, and I had to learn how to swim in it by propelling myself forward with the fluke. By the end of the shoot I was sporting abs of steelhead. (Okay, that's a kind of trout, but you get the idea.)

For purposes of continuity (what little of it there was between the film and TV versions), I was to be transformed into a blonde. The ridiculously thick hair with which I had been blessed/cursed was to be forcibly sequestered under a long wig. The prospect of subduing my wild shoulder-length mane every morning was enough to make even the most seasoned hair wrangler blanch. An obvious solution was agreed upon and my hair was unceremoniously hacked off.

Once my hastily achieved bob was completed (and my eyebrows were bleached), the professionals were charged with the task of figuring out the "bosom situation." Decency—and the censors—demanded a modest, yet topless, mermaid. After an irritating day of what seemed like half the crew gluing, adjusting, squinting, readjusting, and Polaroiding, an ingenious solution was created. Basically, what looked like two flesh-colored yarmulkes were glued to my bosom, and strategically arranged hanks of my flowing blond wig were glued to each of them. Yowch. What no one, least of all I, had failed to imagine was the effect the nightly removal of said contraptions would have on my skin. I had to wear my bra in the shower for the next month. Glamorous.

The first half of the shooting schedule took place at the Disney Studios in Burbank. The second half would be shot at the brand-new MGM/Disney studio in Orlando. In fact, *Splash, Too* would be the first project ever to shoot there, and they were still building around us as we worked. In preparation for the company move to our Florida location, I was half-taught how to scuba in the swimming pool built for *Down and Out in Beverly Hills* on the back lot. Half-taught, because "actual" mermaids don't require oxygen tanks, much less masks. However, learning to "buddy breathe" would come in more than handy twenty-five feet down in Epcot Center's Living Seas attraction.

The system entailed my relying on a safety diver, who remained just out of the shot, holding my oxygen. I realized that achieving my seemingly impossible childhood dream of growing up to be a mermaid had nothing to do with wishing upon a star. It would necessitate me swimming (legs bound and literally sewn into a latex and urethane fin), acting (such as I could), and holding my breath underwater without panicking or expiring until the director called "cut." Mind you, I was required to blithely swim about in the company of sawfish, sea turtles, and a couple of seven-foot tiger sharks while disguised from the *pupek* down as a lovely piece of Nova lox.

The trickiest part of filming was the "wide shot" designed to establish Madison's surroundings. The surprising buoyancy of my tail would cause me to float upward out of the shot. The solution: to pack my tail—so to speak—with ballasting weights to compensate for any bothersome air pockets. It is actually surprising that there were any air pockets left, considering the incontinental drift that occurred every so often during my confinement in that sucker. As Dr. Seuss aptly put it, "Oh, the places you'll go." All but lashed to the faux ocean floor and helplessly dependent on the kindness of others for my next breath, I took a moment to reconsider my vocation . . . What? And give up *show business?*

In the summer of 1989, I auditioned for a movie entitled *3000,* for which I was given only a small section of the script to peruse prior to my reading for Garry Marshall. The part was that of a bitchy Rodeo Drive saleslady, and Garry liked the way I did it. I have no idea what I did or how I did it, as usual. Auditions always cause me varying degrees of short-term memory loss.

He asked me to take a look at another scene, to go out into the waiting room and work on this new character, and come back in when I was ready. I told him I would just like to read it now if that was okay. I always do better with what is known as a "cold-reading." Even five minutes alone with a scene can sabotage me. Left to my own devices, I tend to overthink myself out of any and all positive instincts.

I did get the second part I tried out for—Elizabeth Stuckey, the snobby, bitchy (note the trend) wife of the leading man's lawyer. I had a handful of scenes, some of which Garry let me improvise with my on-screen husband. By the time the movie came out, it had been lightened up a bit in tone, and judging by the amount of yours truly that ended up on the editing room floor, shortened in length. And the picture also had a new title: *Pretty Woman*. Working with Richard Gere and Julia Roberts, to the extent that I did, was a blast. Julia was nice enough; I was a faint blip on her radar, but I didn't expect anything more. Richard was a little more fun. Aside from the fact that he was entertaining to just look at, he was very charming on the set.

Richard and I had a quick on-screen exchange during the polo scene. Curious about this odd girl that he has chosen to bring to this highfalutin event, Elizabeth asks Edward, "Where ever did you find her?" I forget what his scripted response was. But after shooting it a couple of times, I told Richard that he should shoot my character down by responding, "1-900-BABE." This was very hip and cheeky at the time—remember, this was before chat rooms and computer dating. The very next take, he said the line I suggested. Garry loved it and came out from behind his monitor to tell us that he was going to use it. Richard was kind enough to give me credit. A quick cut of that exchange was used in the movie trailer montage. After the movie came out, I came across an actual ad for 1-900-BABE in the back of *LA Weekly*. I had inadvertently inspired a sex chat line. So proud. So very, very proud.

During a much-needed break during filming of that marathon scene, Richard requested a restroom break. I had the same idea and was relieved to know I would soon be relieved. I had realized earlier on in my career that it is always best to wait until the star of the movie needs to go. Ancillary actors who hold up the shoot because they have to "ten-one-hundred"—which is production speak for leaving the set to use the toilet—are thought of less than kindly.

We walked together across the Burbank Equestrian Center lawn pretty much in silence. We glanced back a couple of times at the production assistant ten feet behind us, talking into her walkie-talkie and estimating for the assistant director, and anybody else with a headset, how long our trip to the toilet would take. This is customary and necessary to maintain the schedule, but it is always slightly jarring, not to mention less than relaxing to know that an entire production crew is wagering whether you're doing number one or number two.

Midway through our long trek across the polo field, Richard took off his jacket and slung it over his shoulder. This was late summer in the San Fernando Valley and it was boiling. Had there been a wardrobe assistant along with us, they would have lunged for his coat in order to preserve its unwrinkled state. Steaming the leading man's linen jacket to ensure that it matches the previously shot scene would eat up more time.

As we were nearing the end of our journey, I noticed that there was only one restroom. We would be taking turns. When I gestured for him to go first, he said, "Thanks, I really have to pee." I smiled, gesturing in his general direction, "It would be my pleasure to hold that for you."

He paused, flashed his famous grin at me, and said, "It's okay. I've been doing it my whole life." As he went into the bathroom and closed the door, I turned to the production assistant, reading her face, and said, "I meant hold his *jacket . . .*"

Even though precious little of our on-screen improvisation actually made the final cut, Garry did let us improvise way more than most directors would ever dare. There's a scene where Jason Alexander and I pull up, bickering at each other, in a brand-new $80,000 DeLorean. Hoping to amplify a pointed barb that my character had just hurled at her husband, upon exiting the passenger side I slammed the door. Unfortunately, I did so with such emphasis (John called this "overfocused performance energy") that the window exploded into a million pieces of safety glass. And Jason and I kept on going with our improvised sniping. This happened to occur while *Entertainment Tonight* was on set taping a segment for their show. Garry made a meal of it for their cameras. I was pretty embarrassed, but nowhere on my resume does it say that I'm NOT a klutz.

chapter 8

No Problem, Child

In September 1989, I was called into Universal Studios to audition for a movie called *Problem Child*. I had met the director, Dennis Dugan, almost a year before while I was visiting a friend on the set of *Sonny Spoon*. While eating dinner with Dennis and the cast, I realized that he was one of the funniest people I had ever met. And according to him, the feeling had been mutual: He later told me that he had written my name on a little piece of paper that night and put it in his pocket, intending to call my agent if the right part came along. This is not an uncommon story in the Biz of Show. The road to unemployment is paved with good intentions. But the fact that he actually followed through all those months later is not so common. It is rare, in fact. I'll always be grateful to Dennis for the most important audition of my life.

All I had to go on was the character description: Flo Healy was a nagging housewife, challenged by her ticking biological clock, but her desire to have a child was decidedly less than maternal; it was all about wanting to be invited to elaborate children's parties for the purposes of social networking. I decided to dress down and not to wear any makeup. Translation: lipstick, blush, eyeliner, eye shadow, and only two coats of mascara—you know, the natural look. I did the audition and felt good about it. Which I can tell you means absolutely nothing. I never know. Never. Well, there was feedback. The producers liked me, but they were concerned that my "look" was not desperate enough for the role. They wanted me to look like I was "trying too hard."

So when I went back for the screen test, I twisted and secured my hair, Cinnabon-style, on top of my head. A style, by the way, Mom always discouraged us Yasbeck girls from wearing. When we did, she was sure to comment that we looked like we were "just off the boat." Whether she was referring to the boat from Ireland (her side) or the boat from Lebanon (Dad's) was never clear. As for the clothes—yes, Ann, I'm writing this part—I dug into a box of hand-me-downs I had recently received from Cincinnati. I discovered a particularly sad blouse that looked as if it had gotten into a fight with a Bedazzler . . . and lost. For that little something extra, I MacGuyvered a pair of Alexis Carrington–inspired shoulder pads from a couple of Always Overnight maxi pads, safely-pinned them in place and . . . perfect. *Desperate? Party of one? Your screen test is ready . . .*

This go-around, I performed a scene that was eventually cut from the movie, where I'm berating my gynecologist in the middle of an exam. I gave it my all. Not once during the entire process had I stopped to think about who would be playing Mr. Healy. I figured if they were auditioning the likes of me, the guy playing the dad was probably of the same echelon, that is, a nearbody (nearly nobody). The day after the screen test I got a phone call from my agent. For some reason, it was the most anxious I'd ever been about a role in a movie. I sat down on the edge of my bed just as she was saying, "You got the part." I remember feeling a little bit wobbly—okay, it was a waterbed, so I may have just been riding a rogue wave. I was so thrilled that I had booked this movie, I felt like I was gonna fall over. And then she said, "It's filming in Dallas and you will be working with John Ritter."

John Ritter. *John Ritter.* I told you it was the most important audition of my life. I remember as she said his name, I had one of those echoic moments. Not déjà vu—almost the opposite, a kind of flash forward. It was kismet-ish, fate-y. Now I'm just making words up.

The first time we met was at Dennis Dugan's house on September 25, 1989, for a read-through of the script. These kinds of things are usually outwardly casual, but the producers and writers are certainly paying close attention to the words and to the actors, being that this is the first time they've had the characters fleshed out and all of the actors there in the flesh for a reading. The cast included Michael Richards from *Seinfeld* as The Bowtie Killer, Michael Oliver as Junior, and full-on movie star Jack Warden as Big Ben. John looked a bit worried when we first met. I came to find out later that he was concerned I was perhaps too young for the role—just the kind of thing you can't appreciate when you're twenty-seven years old, like complaining when you're carded in a bar.

On the set of *Problem Child*, I got to witness the master at work. My set call was always an hour before everybody else's. The extra time was needed to tease and shellac Flo's hair into the kind of infrastructure that only Marge Simpson could appreciate. Every morning, a jolt went through me when I would hear John's voice; the trailer door would swing open and John would say "Stepping up!" It's a lovely courtesy most actors forget to employ upon entering. It alerts hair and makeup artists wielding hot and/or pointy objects that the entire rig may be dipping toward the door a bit. On the set of *Problem Child*, "stepping up" also meant *Let the fun begin*. As brilliant a comedian as John was, he was an equally brilliant human. He exuded so much natural charm that he probably could have gotten away with just showing up. Instead, he would wear himself out energizing the set with his sense of fun. Always working, always on, and always enjoying himself.

Anytime John and I had the opportunity, we would seek out Jack Warden, who played John's dad in the movie. He was never hard to find. He could usually be found sitting on the steps of his trailer with the door wide open, smoking a cigar. Jack told us that he had become claustrophobic during his time in the navy, and being inside the trailer with the door closed reminded him too much of the inside of a submarine. John always knew just the right questions to ask to get Jack going.

Jack and John had one particular running bit that lasted through both *Problem Child* and *Problem Child 2*. They would talk to each other on the set in some kind of comedy shorthand, calling out play numbers to each other, as if they were referring to a well-known joke catalog. Right before the director would call action, Jack would bellow from out of nowhere, "Johnny Boy! Bring it on home with a number fourteen on this take." Occasionally, Jack would squat just off camera, but still in John's eye line, and throw him signals as if he was a catcher. Whatever John would do on a take, Jack would pretend that it had infuriated him. "I wanted you to *bunt* . . . IDIOT!" None of this hijinks got in the way of making the film. For all the messing around these guys did in between the scenes, the moment "action" was called they would snap into character and deliver like the consummate professionals they were.

I, on the other hand, was not able to transition quite so smoothly—or at all. John made me laugh so much I kept losing my place. A couple of times when Dennis would call action, I would still be reeling inside my head from whatever John had just said or done. After a queasy pause, I would snap into reality and begin my line. "Cut!" I finally got called on the carpet for being a goof. This was the story of my life.

Growing up, my brother Jay prided himself on being able to whip me up into a frothy craze. Being twelve years older, and about three feet taller than I was, he would get me going by teasing the heck out of me, then nimbly dancing around just out of my reach. God I wanted to slap him. He was funny, fast, and slippery. He did a magnificent Muhammad Ali impression, where he would float like a butterfly and sting like a skinny white bee. He would get me going to the extent that I was literally bouncing off the walls, and then just laugh and hold on to my head with his arm stretched straight out, while I fruitlessly swung away at him with my short arms. I was a Tang-fueled junkyard dog on a short leash. At a time of his choosing, Jay would simply trash talk and shadowbox backward all the way out the door, infuriatingly maintaining eye contact and effortlessly swatting me away like I was a gnat. The door would close and I'd turn back toward the room, panting and wild-eyed, like the Yaz-manian Devil, usually to find my mother standing, arms crossed, Pall Mall in hand, shaking her head in exasperation. I had fallen victim once again. "Ignore him," she would say slowly and deliberately, as if overenunciating the words would help her advice penetrate my thick six-year-old skull this time. How could I ignore him? Jay Yasbeck was the Harlem Globetrotters and I was the basketball. We needed each other.

The day I was finally called aside by the director on the set of *Problem Child,* and nicely asked to *please pull my shit together,* I looked over at John, who was entertaining the teamsters by doing spit-takes. I realized *uh-oh*—this was another boy who was going to be impossible to ignore.

chapter 9

....

Wake Up and Smell the '90s

My first sitcom experience finally arrived in 1990, play-ing John's pregnant wife on *The Cosby Show*. Like the wise folks who brave their first skydive lashed to the front of their trainer, I was not taking any chances. I was taking my first plunge not only strapped to John Ritter but also under the benevolent gaze of Bill Cosby, two undisputed sitcom masters.

The "four-camera half-hour" genre is like no other. Desi Arnaz developed it in 1951 so *I Love Lucy* could be per-formed like a play and filmed like a movie, simultaneously. Lucille Ball's brilliant physical comedy could be captured by four angles at once, while retaining the immediacy of live theater. It was a forty-year-old, tried-and-true format, but it was still pretty intimidating to me. The anticipation of ig-noring the audience and playing to them at the same time, while hitting my marks for four cameras, would have completely unnerved me had I not been working with John. Little did I know, I was jumping out of a plane without a parachute.

My character on the episode was at the end of her pregnancy, and John's character was a high school basketball coach. Dr. Huxtable attempted to counsel and prepare us for the birth, but we ignored him, thinking we knew it all. We were confident that using my husband's high school basketball coaching techniques and our trusted new-age birthing book would suffice.

The scene started with John assuring Dr. Huxtable that we would be fine without his sage advice. John was sitting next to me across the desk from Dr. Huxtable in his office. On "action," he would stand up with the book in hand and walk around the desk, really close to Bill, and say the line, "Everything from conception to birth is in this book."

Seemed easy enough, but for whatever reason, on the first take John said, "Everything from birth to conception is in this book." Cosby laughed. The director, Jay Sandrich, called "Cut!" assuming that John knew he had blown the line by transposing the words. *Wrong.* Take two, he said the same thing. The first few times, it didn't dawn on John why it was wrong. I guess when he learned the script, he had transposed those two words and he'd been practicing his mistake all week in his head. Naturally, on show night, it just came out that way.

When Cosby pointed out the flub to him, an uncharacteristically serious look flashed across John's face. Then he mugged a sheepish grin and shuffled, shoulders down, back to his starting mark in the chair next to me. Take after take, for some reason, he could not get the line out as written. Struggling, in any way, on a sitcom set was so rare an occurrence for John that I think it started messing with his mind. Even though Cosby, whom he idolized, loved it, and the crowd was rooting for him, John was clearly pissed at himself.

After take ten, another misfire, he slunk back to sit in the chair next to me to start the scene over, yet again. I leaned into him and said, in what John would forever refer to as my "full-on Ohio volume," "Jesus, John, you are sweatin' like a *pig*." Through the film and TV work that I had previously done, I had become accustomed to being wired for sound. On a film set, an audible moment of self-reflection or an off-color joke between actors draws, at best, a distant twitter from the direction of an off-camera sound cart hidden behind a bush. That night at the Astoria Studios in Queens, I was introduced to the concept of an unnoticed boom microphone and a live audience. I was nearly knocked over by the initial group gasp, and the ensuing waves of laughter. Had I not been sitting down it would've sat me down.

The assistant director called for "Makeup!" and I mouthed "Oops." I remember searching John's face for any hint that he was angry at me. All I found there was him beaming back at me and shaking his head from side to side. Luckily, my outburst and the ensuing kerfuffle served not only as a distraction but as an unintentional rebooting of his comedy computer. We flew through the rest of the scene undaunted, aside from the audience's protracted standing ovation when John finally spit out the line correctly.

The first half of the '90s became for me a welcome walk through *TV Guide*. I happily found myself working, albeit one week at a time, with some of my favorite actors, including Dixie Carter. I guested on *Designing Women,* where I got to play a ridiculously self-absorbed night nurse charged with looking after Julia Sugarbaker after her hysterectomy. All our scenes took place in a hospital room set built on the edge of the stage. A couple of times, I kind of lost my place during rehearsal because I was mesmerized by Dixie's absolutely elegant and precise comedic delivery, even as she lay there in a hospital gown.

Bob Saget and I guest-starred together on an episode of *Quantum Leap,* playing two-thirds of a 1950s nightclub comedy trio along with the show's star, Scott Bakula. It was one solid week of trying not to break up on camera. As funny as Saget is—and believe me, he is—Bakula killed me.

I had been a Chris Elliott fan ever since his days on *Late Night with David Letterman.* When he got his own series, *Get a Life,* I was praying for a part. When I finally got one, I realized I was on one of the most surreal sitcoms to ever come down the pike. I played a pharmacist who was obsessed with and stalks Chris's character, a paperboy, who has been accidentally run over by a gorgeous doctor played by Emma Samms, with whom he has become obsessed and has begun to stalk. You had to be there . . . and I was!

Guest-starring on a television series is a lot like being a foreign exchange student. Some of the locals are going to be mildly interested in your presence, a few will genuinely give a crap about you, and the rest will multiply you by zero. It's their turf and you are going to be back out auditioning at the end of the episode. I quickly realized that it was in my best interest to just do my job, keep to myself, and quietly sit in my set chair in between scenes. Okay, not technically *my* set chair but *a* set chair with the word CAST stenciled on it. Good enough.

The highlight of my early '90s guest-star-a-palooza was getting to work with two of my TV icons, Andy Griffith and Angela Lansbury. I actually guest-starred on two *Matlock*s and a *Murder, She Wrote*. I got very little screen time with Andy on those two episodes, due to the fact that I didn't play the murderer in either one. I never got to do the sweating-in-the-witness-box scene while Ben Matlock gives me a good old-fashioned country lawyer grillin'. Most of my off-camera time was spent hiding in my trailer to avoid the aimless wandering and snack table grazing for which guest actors are known.

When I was cast in *Murder, She Wrote*, I played the whiny daughter-in-law in a big Italian family. It was a giant cast with lots of guest stars. The entire week of shooting I was lost in the magical Lansburyness of the situation in which I found myself. I tried to stay sequestered as much as possible, so I wouldn't come off as a big, hovering dork of a fan. Luckily, one of the scenes took place around an enormous dining room table. The dinner scene must have included at least ten actors and I had only a couple of lines, so I was not stressing out at all. Shooting a scene with characters around a table means you're in it for the long haul. One-hour dramas use one camera, like in film; shooting the establishing shot and then shooting all the individual points of view, plus any other angle the director wants to use, always makes for a marathon day. I was stuck. During these kinds of "seatbelt moments," I can't get away with my usual antics. I am impeded, logistically or otherwise, from being my usual squirmy self. On that day it worked in my favor. Being "trapped" for hours at that dining room table with Angela Lansbury was heavenly—as if part of me was on that Universal Studios soundstage, and the other part was back in 1971, gazing up at her in *Bedknobs and Broomsticks* at the Jolly Roger Drive-in.

In 1992, John starred with Markie Post in the CBS sitcom *Hearts Afire.* This is also where he met his good buddy, Billy Bob Thornton. From the start Billy and John had a very quirky chemistry. At a political fund-raiser before the show was in production, Billy, sporting a long, skinny ponytail, walked over, grabbed John's hand, and introduced himself. Using the twangiest, countriest, good ole boy voice he could affect, he said, "I b'lieve I'm gonna be workin' wich ya'll on that there *Hearts Afire.* I'm Billy Bob."

John paused then said, ". . . Um, yeah . . . nice to meet you . . ." then proceeded to pull himself together and sincerely engage this odd guy in conversation. After a few exchanges, Billy let down the façade and said in his regular voice, "I'm just messing with you, John. But it is nice to meet you."

John knew that, in terms of improv, he had just met his match. A good quarter of their off-camera dialogue on the set was an elaborate goof. During the run of *Hearts Afire,* these two guys gained enormous respect for each other's dedication to creating characters and inhabiting them. The role of Vaughn Cunningham that Billy wrote for John in the screenplay of *Sling Blade* showed that he clearly had confidence in the depth of John's talent. John was so proud to be part of that movie. John loved to say that Billy Bob was nominated for Best Adapted Screenplay along with a young guy named Arthur Miller.

During the filming of *Hearts Afire*, John and Markie Post were asked to present the Horatio Alger Award in Washington, D.C. We decided to extend the trip by flying to New York to see Jerry Lewis in *Damn Yankees*. John and I and Markie and her husband, Michael Ross, were drunk with Jerry Lewis-ness the entire trip. As jazzed as we all were, I know nobody could have been as excited as John. He made no secret of the fact that Jerry had changed his life. His passion for comedy as a kid was stoked by the *Martin & Lewis* comedy hour and films. He knew and loved everything about them. The fact that John's dad, Tex, never *got* Jerry made him all the more appealing. John was more than well-versed in Martin and Lewis history. We still have an enormous video and book collection that he amassed over the years.

For John, Jerry Lewis was his mentor. They had never met, but John had felt a bond with him ever since the first time he laid eyes on him on screen. No Jerry Lewis legend or lore was lost on John. He ate it up like he was a one-man France. He could go on and on about Jerry's revolutionary comedic style. He would expound, hilariously imitating him, on why and how Jerry Lewis was funny, noting how, being taller than Dean, he had to work in a crouch for all those years. John had also, like Jerry, devoted himself to charity, by way of his own telethon for United Cerebral Palsy.

Now the four of us were on our way to see *Damn Yankees*, and John could not stop debating whether or not he should try to go backstage to see his comedic idol. He was never one to assume other actors wanted him to visit backstage after the performance. He always thought it came off a little weird, like, "Hey, fellow thespian, just thought I'd stop backstage so you could meet me." He didn't really go for that. When John was in the audience, he just wanted to be an audience member. But this time it was Jerry. So John brought a bottle of Champagne to the show with a little note of congratulations. When we got to the theater, he sent it back to the stage manager. He sat through the first act enjoying the hell out of himself, but also feeling a bit like a dopey stage-door Johnny. When intermission came, a woman began inching down our row with a big smile on her face. She leaned into John and said, "Mr. Lewis would like you and your group to come backstage after the show." John held my hand and squeezed it for the entire second half of the play.

After the show, the four of us were escorted backstage. We really were just like four goofy fans. Before we walked into the dressing room, John turned me toward him, hands on my shoulders, and said very seriously, "I love you, Amy." I remember thinking at the time that it sounded a lot like the beginning of "I love you, Amy—but I love Jerry Lewis more. Please find it in your heart to be happy for us." I suppose it was actually just his attempt to steady himself on that momentous occasion in time.

With John leading the way, Markie, Michael, and I filed into the dressing room. Jerry was resplendent in his robe, still glowing, figuratively and literally, from his tour de force performance as The Devil. He welcomed us with such hospitality I felt like I was going to cry. At one point, he put his arm around John and walked him over to a picture that was hanging on the wall. John glanced back at us for a moment—just in time to catch me palming a Kleenex from the dressing table with a smudge of Jerry's deep tan pancake makeup on it and jamming it into my cleavage.

John told him that we were going to Sardi's—the iconic Broadway restaurant—for a late dinner and we would love it if he could join us. He said that the cast was raising money for Broadway Cares by signing programs for donations after the show, but he would try to drop by if he could. On our way to the car, we saw a long line of fans waiting patiently to have their moment with Jerry. John broke away from us and cut in line, shushing the fans who recognized him so they wouldn't spoil the joke. He got down on his knees and shuffled forward a little bit at a time, making his way up to the table. When it was his turn, he pushed his program across the table, and in a Jerry voice said, "Could you possibly sign my program, Mr. Jerry Lewis, if it isn't too much trouble for you? Hmmm? Hmmm?" Face-to-face with a whining, four-foot-tall John Ritter, it took Jerry a few moments to comprehend what he was seeing. But the minute he did, he was completely into the bit. Patting John on the head like he was an annoying little fan, he said, "Sure, kid," and then they both put their faces very close to the program as Jerry, biting his tongue with mock concentration, signed his name.

We all said our good-byes and then rode, electrified by our experience, to Sardi's. We were famished but having a hard time ordering because we were all kinds of crazed by what we had just experienced. Markie and I excused ourselves from the table and never stopped yakking all the way upstairs to the ladies room and into our respective stalls. As we were finishing up our business and still jabbering like we were at the prom, we heard an impossibly familiar wail. "LAAAADIES!!!!!" Jerry had made a grand entrance into Sardi's, made his way to our table, and asked, "Where are the girls?" John and Michael pointed, dumbfounded, in the general direction of upstairs. Jerry turned on his heels and instantly transitioned into his signature pigeon-toed walk. He made his way up the stairs to fetch us, followed by the boys and more than a few restaurant patrons and staff.

John recounted that moment over and over again to me. From his point of view, he could see Jerry leaning in the doorway of the restroom screaming for us LAAAAADIES to come out. He said that we emerged red-faced (dare I say, flushed), squealing and reeling like teenage Beatles fans. He also swore that I *swooned* and landed in Jerry's arms. The hijinks continued downstairs in the restaurant, where John and Jerry performed an elaborate closing-up-the-place-for-the-night bit. Kicking people out of their seats and stacking chairs on the table as if oblivious to the chaos they were creating, Ritter and Lewis brought the house down.

I came by my love of Mel Brooks, like many of my generation, by way of a weekly indoctrination booster shot called *Get Smart*. I also caught bits and pieces of his work through reruns of his movies on television and began associating the name Mel Brooks with "flat-out funny." I was too young in 1974 to see *Blazing Saddles* on the big screen.

But my brother and sister's faithful re-creation of the camp-fire scene in all of its flatulent glory, spoke directly to my already warped sense of humor. By the time eighth grade had rolled around, I was in the back row of a dark movie theater having my first and only cigarette with Judy Mongan, while we laughed our butts off watching *Young Frankenstein*. I quickly became a young devotee of Brooksian humor.

In 1992, the casting call went out for the role of Maid Marion in Mel Brooks's *Robin Hood: Men in Tights*. They were seeking a twentysomething, busty, virginal, British blonde. Obviously, I was not on the list because . . . let's go with . . . I wasn't blonde? Luckily, after they had seen all of the appropriate prospects, they widened their search to include the likes of me. Instead of the usual clip reel that features a compilation of an actor's finest moments, my agents sent a tape of my appearance on *The Tonight Show* with Johnny Carson. It worked. They called me in to read for the part.

I have never been so focused on anything as I was when John helped me with my audition the night before my meeting. He was giving me brilliant notes and really opening up his comic magician's bag of tricks for me. As the night went on, I began to entertain myself by asking him to demonstrate this move or that one. Experiencing John Ritter as Maid Marion as retold by Mel Brooks was very satisfying. He was quite good. My favorite bit was when he pretended the sweet little blue bird on his finger began to attack him like he was Tipi Hedren in *The Birds*. He even rattled the script pages to affect the sound of the crazed bird's wings.

The next morning, I added the finishing touches to my audition outfit. I stuffed my bra—well, my NEW bra: the 36D that the saleslady at Bullocks Wilshire tried to kindly dissuade me from buying. ("Sweetie, you *may* want to try that on . . .") Knee socks, mittens, everything that came in pairs went in there. I even figured out how to affect cleavage. My boobs met for the first time, hitting it off immediately.

The morning started off with a surprise. The usually surly guard at the gate of the Warner Hollywood studio happily waved me through and personally pointed out a prime parking spot. I had failed to throw on a sweater over my barely believable décolletage—also known as my VIP parking pass. Once inside the audition room, performing my scenes on camera, I had a surprising amount of *fun*—a word I don't typically associate with auditioning. Maid Marion with a dash of John Ritter was a joy to attempt. I even did my version of the killer bird bit. I had no idea if anything came across the way I had intended, but I would know soon enough, as they would be showing the tape to Mel later that day.

When I got a call back to come in and meet with the man himself, I panicked a little. Getting dressed, I struggled to re-create the bosom. I should have made a chart. Meeting Mel Brooks was a dream come true. We did the two scenes that he had pulled from his script. Then he gave me some direction and I did it again. He liked the combination of my syrupy upper-crust accent and my Borsht Belt humor. Referencing one the most elegant actresses of all time, Mel said, "I like you. You're like Deborah Kerr with a little old Jewish man inside."

I kidded him: "Well, it won't be you, so don't get any ideas."

The next day I was home in my Century City condo and I got the call every actor would die to get: "I have Mr. Brooks on the phone for you, please hold . . ."

I sat down.

"Amy? Don't leave town. Don't cut your hair." He told me I had the part and began laying out the Maid Marion character in full for me. I couldn't breathe. I was memorizing every nuance of every word he said. I was sure that when I saw John later that night, I would be so excited to tell him that I would forget something. I didn't. Especially interesting to John was the exchange Mel and I had about the bathtub scene. Maid Marion stands up in the tub to dry off only to reveal that she is sporting an "Everlast" chastity belt. Mel was very reassuring about the minimal amount of skin that would be showing.

"We may just glimpse the *side* of your bosom."

How was I going to say this?

"Mel, they don't have sides, exactly . . ."

"Hmm?"

"Nice *fronts,* neither of which will ever be seen on screen, but no *sides* to speak of, no . . ."

I told him the truth about the stuffing. He took it well. I told him my idea of doing what I had done in *Splash, Too* with a twist. Instead of flesh colored pasties we could glue on *lady boobs.* He went for it and the rest is *her*story.

I laughed through every day on that movie. Even when Mel would get frustrated with us and bark at us like he we were his soldiers at the Battle of the Bulge. We would all breathe a collective sigh of relief when he would follow up his call of "Cut!" by adding, "Surprisingly good! Print!" On days when I would be done shooting before the rest of the cast, I couldn't bring myself to leave. I would sign out and then change back into my casual attire, and spend the rest of the day sitting near Mel; watching him direct and goading him into telling stories. Heaven. Just heaven.

chapter 10

John-Foolery

Here's how you crack up a dark, crowded movie theater. You ready? You sit there and wait for a lull in the action. You choose your moment and then pipe up with: *"You're sorry? You're sorry? You throw up on my date and you say you're sorry?"* And then you just sit back and wait for the laughter to subside, if it ever does. I can personally vouch for the effectiveness of this one.

John was a firm believer in random public displays of silliness. Whenever he could get away with it—usually with little regard for the appropriateness of the venue—John would launch into an extended improvisation. The elevator scenes were typically the most intense for me. It's always nice to add a touch of claustrophobia to your potentially humiliating, involuntary participation in public theater. I always dreaded those extended rides up and down in tall buildings.

The setup was always the same. And it only worked if we started out alone. All would be fine—just John and me to-gether riding up in the elevator—until I would feel it start to slow to a stop. I knew that as soon as the doors opened and admitted an unsuspecting citizen, John would become somebody else. Under my breath I would always say, "Please don't, please don't, please don't, please don't, please don't." He would move to the other side of the car before the person entered, and—as is common social practice—the pas-senger wouldn't make eye contact with either one of us. But then John would just start talking to me across the elevator, ignoring the newcomer. He would pull his baseball cap way down over his eyes and start speaking up in a semicreepy voice with stuff like: "You sure are purdy . . ." I would ignore him but he would keep it up. "Um . . . Lady . . . you smell good . . ." until I would be forced to answer. I would usually reply with something like, "Sir, I am really going to need you to stop talking to me now." Kind of a compro-mise, walking the line between blowing the improvisation—which seemed like high treason—and letting him know how freaking uncomfortable it made me.

Our fellow riders would scoot subtly—or not so subtly—closer and closer to the front of the elevator until their noses were practically crow-barring the doors open. When their floor number lit up they would escape. It was always a rush. And at least the innocent bystander had an interesting story to tell once they got to their destination.

He had been doing that kind of stuff his whole life. And he would pull anybody he was with into the improvisation. It was actually quite thrilling, but we would just have to trust

John, the Man in Charge. He was at the controls and we all were more than happy to just be along for the ride.

With John, a nice meal at a restaurant always came with a side of comedy. When the waiter would first approach the table, John would invariably say, "Okay . . . let's see . . . fried calamari all around . . ." I don't know why that tickled him so much. I guess just seeing the waiter sincerely start to write it down as the rest of the table was protesting. Hundreds of meals started exactly like that. And for some reason, it seems like he always managed to catch us off guard. He was a tireless and devoted practitioner of the running gag.

John never failed to test the bounds of what other people considered funny. And restaurants provided ample opportunity for humor. At least once during every meal there would come a moment when, rapt with attention, we would all be leaning forward to hear the punch line of a joke or the climax of a story, when John would notice that a patron or two was straining to hear what he had to say. He would always break the moment by slapping his hands down on the table and loudly announcing to us, "And *that*, kids, is how Burt Reynolds got away with murder."

My favorite restaurant antic had to do with the fact that—here comes an understatement—John ate quickly. His plate would be clean before anybody else at the table was halfway through their meal. Many were the times an unsuspecting waiter, trying to be funny, would comment on this and innocently cross the border into Opposite World. Deftly employing his unique brand of comedy judo, John would use his opponent's attempt at humor against him. The waiter, expecting his surefire line to be met by John and his entire table with a satisfied chuckle, would soon realize, to his dismay, that he had entered . . . *The Irony-Free Zone.*

WAITER (SPYING JOHN'S EMPTY PLATE): "Ooooh, I see you didn't like the pasta at all, Mr. Ritter."

JOHN: "No, I actually really enjoyed it."

WAITER (SMIRKING): "Right, I know, I was making a jo—"

JOHN: "But you said that I didn't like it—"

WAITER (NOT SMIRKING): "I was just trying to be funny—"

JOHN: "—when in fact, I *loved* it."

WAITER (AS IF TO A MORON): "Again, Mr. Ritter, I was only joking because your plate is empty—"

JOHN: "Exactly! Which *proves* I really liked it!"

WAITER (A LITTLE AFRAID): "Why don't I just clear that plate for you—"

JOHN: "Oh, God—*promise* me you won't go back in the kitchen and break that chef's heart by telling him I didn't like his pasta."

WAITER (AFRAID): "Why would . . . ? Okay, I promise."

JOHN: "Thank you."

WAITER: "Would you like a refill on your Diet Coke?"

JOHN: "What the FUCK is that supposed to mean?!"

John was pretty comfortable everywhere he went; he had his share of savoir faire. I think the reason for that is because he was himself wherever he went. He was always appropriate, exhibiting the perfect manners his mother Dorothy had wisely taught both her boys. Somehow, though, he always managed to have fun and make sure that you had fun, too. No matter what the event or how austere the occasion, you could be sure that John would have you doubled over with laughter at some point. He could not *not* be entertaining. It wasn't an ego thing. Maybe it did have something to do with control, to some degree, but it wasn't manufactured power. It was real. John was a leader that way. He walked in a room, assessed it, and basically created his own weather. Very seldom did a person escape his charisma. Luckily for us; that was just who the guy was and how he related to the world.

Nothing is more fascinating than someone who is fascinated by you. (Am I revealing too much about myself?) John was absolutely fascinated by people—their interactions, their conflicts, their egos, and their tenderness. He was a keen observer and he stored it all somewhere. Who knows where? He called on this catalog of character traits and physicality with DSL speed. Generalized information and the teeniest, tiniest quirks were all grist for his mill. He would create and re-create dozens of characters just for our and his own enjoyment every day.

John's grateful audience, including all of us who knew him best, were happy to be observers of his ongoing performance. We were fascinated by him. Thrilled to be with him and be entertained. But in truth, he was our audience. He studied and scrutinized our every move. Every smile. Every grimace. Every wince.

He came to relish the sporadic stretches of anonymity that a beard or baseball cap or just dumb luck afforded him. He was obviously grateful for the respite from the glaring spotlight of fame that those times provided him. But more important, he would make the most of those rare moments to observe people as he had in his childhood, without being observed.

His intentions were twofold. John absolutely found sincere and sacred joy in witnessing the eternal glory of man. On the other hand, Mr. Physical Comedy did have to restock the old bag of tricks now and again. The *keen but kind* scrutiny to which he subjected us was necessary for his process. In performance after performance, John drew on his observations, artfully blending the common behaviors that connect us all and the peculiarities that set us apart. Possessing both qualities, commonality and individuality, is what makes humans human. Seeing our humanity—at once unique and universal—reflected in the mirror that John held up to us was always a revelation. And he was as entertained by us as we were by him. We were a joy to imitate for the inimitable John Ritter.

His observations made him a firm believer that it's not necessarily the fall or the mistake or the misstep or the slight that's the funny part. It's the recovery that is so recognizable to us. Trying to maintain one's dignity in the most undignified of situations is a common human denominator.

If you notice, that's always the funniest part on *America's Funniest Home Videos*. Tom Bergeron was a dear friend of John's and they shared a similar sense of humor. Listening to John and Tom go on about some of the videos on the show was priceless. They agreed that the comic gold is always caught on camera in those few extra moments after the impact. It's then that you see the person desperately trying to pull it together. "I meant to do that, I meant to hit myself in the balls with a bat." It's the same impulse people have after tripping and falling: they get up and glance back disapprovingly at an empty spot on the sidewalk. That damn invisible banana peel! Clearly, they are way too cool to have completely dorked out for no reason. John believed that about 90 percent of our time as beings on this earth is spent maintaining a modicum of poise. To his way of thinking, the only antidote was to embrace your inner goofball and get it over with.

So next time you're in a fancy-ish restaurant and your waiter brings over that ornate silver dessert tray for your perusal, get real close to the selections as if you can't decide, and then rear back your head and let loose a gigantic sneeze. It's best if you move your head around like you are blowing out birthday candles to make sure the spray is evenly distributed over the entire display. Then make a space on the table in front of you, tuck your napkin in your collar, and say, "Well, I guess you can just leave that here now."

chapter 11

Ninety-Something

It was 1994 and the New Year came in with a bang . . . and a rumble . . . and a crash. The morning of January 17, we were asleep at John's Coldwater Canyon house when we were rudely awakened. When you live in Southern California, earthquakes come with the territory. From time to time, the *territory* literally quakes. This was a big one. Not *the* big one. But *a* big one.

There was no electricity, so we went into the garage and started up his car to listen to the news reports pouring in from all over the city. Forcing the disabled garage door open, we backed out onto the street. As we drove to my apartment in Century City, we surveyed the damage along the way, most of it mild to medium. When we got to my building, John insisted on walking with me up the eleven floors to my place. Before opening the door I took a deep breath, not knowing what we'd find inside. I was relieved to see that even though my shelves had fallen down and all of my dishes had crashed to the floor, the damage was minor.

The high-rises in Los Angeles have all been retrofitted in case of earthquakes. They are built to sway so they don't topple. I couldn't imagine what it would have been like for my neighbors on the eleventh floor earlier that morning.

Before John left to check in on everybody else, he walked down the little hall at the back of my apartment to check out the damage in my office. He turned around, came right back out, and closed the door behind him. "Honey, do not go in there. It is a disaster area. It will break your heart. Everything is everywhere. It's too much." He wanted to go through the wreckage with me and help me restore my office to its former glory. I promised him I wouldn't go in without him.

Of course, the moment he left, I went in.

And it was exactly as I had left it the night before. Actually, that room had sustained the least damage of my whole place. I guess John had never really looked in my office before that morning. Oops. Never did fess up.

Growing up, every so often my mom would work up the steam to make the arduous journey up the stairs to my room. She would always come down shaking her head in exasperation, "Looks like a damn tornado hit it." At least here in California, I could blame an earthquake and get away with it.

The earthquake must have also created some sort of a crack in the Earth that caused acting jobs to ooze up and seep into Hollywood. In 1994 the work really began to pick up. Even though I did not spring from a show business family, I did get to play the daughter of a few of my absolute comedy idols. I was cast as Harry Anderson's sister-in-law on *Dave's World*, and my mother was played by none other than Mrs. Brady herself, Florence Henderson.

When I was a kid, I lived for that Friday night comedy block: *The Brady Bunch* and *The Partridge Family* were absolutely part of who we were in my generation. Aside from ABC afterschool specials and my squirreled away copy of *Are You There, God? It's Me, Margaret,* it was the parents on those shows who provided me with life lessons. My family, my school, and the Catholic Church were not completely unhelpful. They were certainly ready at all times with plenty of answers. I just never felt that my brand of prepubescent questions, of which I had an inexhaustible supply, were safe to ask. Even though these early '70s sitcoms portrayed a "family hour" version of preteen angst, I was able to glean more information from them than I could have ever tapped into at home.

I found Mrs. Brady especially cool. She was a survivor. She was bringing up three very lovely girls, she was a newlywed (with a hot, curly permed husband), and she was a kickass stepmom. I could picture myself in the Brady kitchen with Marcia and Jan, asking our mom, Carol, questions about menstruation and sex—whispering, of course, because god forbid Cindy should overhear. Long as I might for that kind of relationship with my mother, it was never going to happen. Part of me must have known that the motherly Brady wisdom was actually being spun by a room full of male writers in Hollywood, but I remained unfazed.

From our first moment together on the *Dave's World*

set, I realized that I was right to pine for Mrs. Brady all those years. Turns out, I was unknowingly pining for Florence Henderson. We hit the ground running as fast friends. We never shut up. We talked and laughed and shared filthy jokes. Filthy. Our scenes together were more than fun for me; I even got to sing an annoying duet of "If Ever I Would Leave You" with her.

My other favorite experience with a television legend was working with Dick Van Dyke on *Diagnosis Murder,* which was as close to the Twilight Zone as I will ever come. He is a hero to me, as he is to any actor who has ever even dabbled in the sitcom genre. He's the master. John absolutely idolized him and was honored to present him with the Comedy Hall of Fame Award in 1994.

As much as *The Dick Van Dyke Show* meant to me, I have to admit that in my heart Dick will always be Caractacus Potts, the father from *Chitty Chitty Bang Bang.* That was all I could think about the entire week. On the last day of shooting the episode, we were on the set in between takes, and he leaned in to thank me for the gift from John that I had left inside his trailer that morning. John had written him a hilarious love note inside the cover of a Calvin and Hobbes cartoon book.

We were face-to-face and his mouth was moving and I was full-on tripping. My worlds had collided. The "That's cool, I'm an actor, just chatting with another actor" world smashed into the "Holy crap! It's Dick Van Dyke!" world. He was in the middle of very sweetly telling me to thank John for him when I just stopped him. I told him I was gonna kick myself for the rest of my life if I didn't ask him something. He looked discernibly worried and then relieved when I said, "Can you please sing a little 'Truly Scrumptious' to me?" And, by God, he did it. Halfway through I chimed/barged in with the counterpoint music box part sung by Sally Ann Howe in the movie. Truly satisfying. I stopped short of asking him to please come over and sing John and me to sleep that night with "Hushabye Mountain."

In 1995, John made a TV movie with Andy Griffith. Tex and Andy had been friends and John was very excited to be working with him. The project was called *Gramps*, and it was about a psycho grandfather. John had always been fascinated by Andy in his pre-Mayberry role of the egomaniacal Lonesome Rhodes in Elia Kazan's *A Face in the Crowd.*

They were filming in North Carolina and South Carolina, and I was in Baltimore filming a small part in *Home for the Holidays,* directed by Jodie Foster. When production was halted for a week while Holly Hunter recovered from the flu, I flew down to North Carolina to be with John. I went to work with him every day for a week and watched his scenes with Andy.

Although I had worked with Andy in the past, playing two different characters on two different episodes of *Matlock,* I had never seen him like this. Evil Andy was riveting. John thoroughly enjoyed their time together off the set as well. I flew back to Baltimore to film my one scene (my one scene was with Holly Hunter, Dylan McDermott, and Robert Downey, Jr., so I'm not complaining), and John got better acquainted with Andy and his wife. He spent a lot of time at their house. So much so, that the Griffiths named a dog after him: Mary Margaret Ritter. Their Christmas card always included a photograph with their dogs, and their holiday greeting always included all of them by name. Nobody enjoyed getting the Griffiths' holiday card more than John. Every year after we were married, he would always make sure to remind me of the irony that Andy's beagle Mary Margaret had taken his last name, but I had declined.

In the summer of 1994, I auditioned for the part of Helen's sister on the sixth season of the NBC sitcom *Wings*. I got the part and was to appear as Casey Chapel Davenport in two episodes, after which the producers had the option of dumping me or picking me up for the rest of my contract. I had to make it work.

Being on a sitcom is the best job in show business. In essence, you rehearse a twenty-two-minute play for a week and then perform it for an audience who already loves you. Luckily, they went ahead and added me to the cast. The big, big, big ole cast: Tim Daly, Stephen Weber, Crystal Bernard, David Schram, Rebecca Schull, Thomas Hayden Church, and Tony Shalhoub. By the time I joined the *Wings* family, they had gotten this sitcom business down to a science. It was a beautiful thing.

I tried to just do my job without much fanfare and observe as much as I could. Flying under the radar is not my strong suit. I really could not play it cool. I was excited to wake up and go to work every morning. The show filmed on the Paramount lot. I loved driving through those gates every day like Norma Desmond. All day long I felt like I *was* John Ritter's *window*. It was as if I were making a movie in my head, of life from my point of view, that I would replay for John: for his amusement, amazement, and I'm not ashamed to admit, approval. Every nuance of my day was reported to him when I came home.

Occasionally, I would be so worked up over the many crazy on-set incidents that I wouldn't know where to start. He would say, "Just give me the headlines." I would do just that, and he would choose which stories he wanted to hear first. Whether it was actor antics, brilliant last-minute rewrites, or craft service kerfuffles, he would listen, engrossed. On the set, I always felt a little like I was sitcom-ing for two. I never felt alone because I knew that even the tiniest of personal triumphs would be exponentially multiplied when I got home and told the story to my rapt audience of one. I was always aware that I was outrageously fortunate to be able to share the daily slings and arrows flying on stage nineteen. I knew that any disappointment or slight I had weathered during my workday would be deftly defused by John's humor, experience, and wisdom. He was my goofy guru and I felt so lucky every day to have him.

We shot *Wings* on Tuesday nights. At the end of the show, we would take our company bow and the pages would escort the audience out the door. For technical or time reasons, there were usually a couple of scenes to be reshot. At the end of the night, the cast would be sent home (or wherever they were convening with the crew for refreshments) with their scripts for the next episode.

I always parked my Miata under a light in the corner of the parking lot. That way I could casually stroll to my car and then, once inside, tear through the next week's script. This is where what John called "bullshit, bullshit, my part" comes in. I would scan the pages for Casey's lines, speed-reading past or all-out skipping everyone else's parts. I know it would've been much cooler to have thrown next week's table draft in the backseat and driven off to the after-show gathering. I just never did it. I usually ended up at Café Luna on Melrose to slam down some pasta puttanesca with my small but faithful band of Tuesday night show-goers.

The shooting schedule had us filming three weeks on and then taking one week off. On show night of the third episode every month, the cast members would be gearing up for their weeklong hiatus. They would share or cagily avoid sharing their plans. All three years that I was on the show, that free week would always throw me. I dreaded it. The "not working" felt too much like "not working." I would be very antsy all hiatus week long until Tuesday night when my new script would get dropped off on John's doorstep. (By then, my Century City apartment had become, in effect, an eleventh-floor storage unit with a view.) John would always be the one to hear the production assistant's car driving away. His ears would perk up and he would practically bolt for the door to retrieve my script. Without fail, he would hand it to me saying, "And not a moment too soon." Mysteriously, my PMS had synched up with my monthly week off and John had, understandably, been conditioned to react to the sound of the P.A.'s car door with unbridled joy. It heralded a welcomed three-week run where steady work and hormones conspired to keep my mood elevated.

As the newest cast member on *Wings*, I was still enthusiastic about doing publicity, but the rest of the cast was all but over it. The on-set interviews with the likes of *Entertainment Tonight* and the other infotainment shows were always fraught with peril. As if slipping up and coming off as a complete idiot were not enough, the random cast members milling about in the background usually had some mischief up their sleeves. Every so often, one of the visiting entertainment shows would pin one of us down to chat about an upcoming episode or an outside project we had going on. For the cast, especially the boys, seeing one of the team being interviewed in the middle of the set usually proved too tempting.

I remember it feeling a lot like knowing a bloated pigeon is hovering tail-first on a ledge just above your patio brunch table. The wary interviewee would be forced to maintain the obligatory on-camera repartee, while remaining acutely aware that a world of crap could raindown on them at any moment. You could be in for taunting, razzing, possible mooning, or any other strategic ego-deflating act of sabotage. It's always a challenge to attempt to sincerely plug your dramatic TV movie while Steve Weber is pantomiming a physically impossible (unless Weber is way more limber than he looks) sexual act directly behind the interviewer's head. Thank God the bulk of publicity for the show was done off set.

Early on, I got a chance to make a dream come true while doing publicity for the show. I got the unbelievably thrilling once-in-a-lifetime chance to fly with the Blue Angels. *Wings* was set in a tiny Nantucket airport, so *Entertainment Tonight* and our show's publicist gave us the opportunity to fly with them in their F-18s. Only two people fit in the jet, the pilot and passenger behind him in the jump seat. I was beyond thrilled—and beyond scared. I had to rearrange my brain temporarily to take on what was, for me, the gargantuan task of completely surrendering control. Trusting the pilot—and let's face it, these guys are the crème de la crème—was the only choice.

Tony Shalhoub, who played Antonio Scarpacci on the show, also went up that day and *Entertainment Tonight* promoted the segment as a battle of the sexes. It was an unbelievably cool experience . . . that I'll never, ever do again. But I stayed in the air a really long time. We flew all of the crazy maneuvers that the Blue Angels usually do in a formation. Things started to slip out once I was upside down and hurtling across the sky at several Gs, including a couple of intense upheavals, gastric as opposed to emotional, along with way too many cries of "Faaaarr oooout!" The outtakes from the jump seat's onboard camera could have been mistaken for a high-altitude episode of *Taxi Cab Confessions*. I confess: I loved it too crazy much.

I can't believe how brave I was. Every once in a while I do something completely out of my comfort zone. And I've come to realize that in most of those instances, I'm actually "showing off," in a way, for my dad. Even though my father died years and years ago, it still feels completely natural to do something for his approval. My dad was an airplane mechanic at Wright Air Force Base in Ohio during World War

II. He worked on gliders and always went up with the pilots on their first test flight. He said that this was their insurance that their mechanic was not doing a half-ass job. When we would go to an amusement park, my dad would always comment that he flew loops and did aerial stunts in the Air Force, but now he couldn't even watch me go around on a merry-go-round for fear he would barf. Going up with the Blue Angels was like a tribute, or more accurately, a communion with him. And the truth is, no matter how you feel intellectually about the concept of heaven, you can't quite help but feel closer to someone who has passed when you are up in the clouds.

In 1995, I got a familiar phone call: "I have Mr. Brooks on the phone for you, please hold . . ." He asked me to play Mina in his horror spoof *Dracula: Dead and Loving It*. I told him he had to meet my *Wings* buddy Steven Weber for the part of Jonathan. Sold! By May, Steve and I were Brooksing it up on the set with Leslie Nielsen and Harvey Korman in *Dracula*, while John was in Arkansas, Billy Bobbing it up on the set of *Sling Blade*. The continuity Polaroids that he sent from the movie were taped on my dressing room mirror. I would come in to find production assistants staring agape at one in particular. Billy had the hair department purposely give John's character, Vaughn Cunningham, a "trying to be chic and juuuust missing . . . by a mile . . . hair cut and highlights." The resulting "pineapple boy" look gave Vaughn the out of place *hair don't* that definitely mirrored his fish out of water circumstances. John loved the effect for the part and sent me the picture.

By that June, when we attended Steve Weber and Juliette Hohnen's wedding in London, his hair had not returned to any semblance of normalcy. When we got to the hotel, John decided to help things along by haphazardly giving himself a haircut with his toenail clippers. When he slunk out of the bathroom with a hotel robe twisted around his head I knew there was trouble. He whipped off his turban and pointed to his head with a big, desperate grin. "Wouldja believe . . . *PUNK*?!" I had known him long enough to believe anything.

Labor Day, 1997: John and I had just moved into our house together and he was fresh from shooting a movie in Canada with Daphne Zuniga and Roddy McDowell called *The Truth About Lying*. Roddy had always loved John and photographed him a couple times for his collection of celebrity portraits. He was kind enough to invite John and me to be his guest at Elizabeth Taylor's Labor Day party that year. Yeah, I said it, Elizabeth Taylor. However many years you've lived in Hollywood, I don't think you could possibly be jaded enough not to be freakin' jumping out of your skin excited to be invited to Liz's house. Surprisingly, John had never met her and God knows I hadn't.

When we arrived, her friends and family were there but she had not made her appearance yet. She was still upstairs being lovingly fussed over by her dear friend and longtime hairdresser, Jose Eber. We wandered around her spacious backyard, trying to inconspicuously swivel and position ourselves to view the star-studded assembly of partygoers. At one point, we were beckoned from across the lawn by a very handsome older man and his gorgeous wife. He had a long gray ponytail, a scruffy beard, and beautiful, piercing brown eyes. We walked toward them and were about five feet away when we both realized that it was Mr. and Mrs. Gregory Peck.

We were both ginormous fans. *To Kill a Mockingbird* and *Gentlemen's Agreement* were two of a handful of films that we shared as our all-time favorites. Mrs. Peck had called us over because she couldn't think of my name, even though I looked familiar to them. When I told them "Amy Yasbeck," they blinked back disappointment. Then we all politely made conversation to fill the awkward moment until the announcement came that brunch was served. Relieved, John and I walked back up to the house and stood in line for the buffet with our white china plates in hands.

Just then, Ms. Taylor made her entrance into the room, absolutely radiant, with Jose at her side (radiant in his own long-haired, cowboy-hat kind of way). She was only six months away from having had surgery to remove a benign tumor from her brain. Her hair was very short and white. Jose had cut and spiked and moussed it into the most gorgeous, perfect meringue imaginable. *This* was a movie star. The lack of her signature black mane only reinforced that it was always all about her face, her eyes.

I remember my mother showing me the picture in *Life* magazine of Elizabeth Taylor with no makeup, her hair up in a towel, and just not being able to get over how beautiful this creature was. And now this beautiful movie star creature had her violet eyes set on John and me and was cutting through the crowd in her own living room. People were practically falling away and bowing as she walked through, making a beeline for us. We both took the plates in our hands and held them up behind each other's heads like halos, and then basically curtsied as she came over. She started laughing uproariously, her eyes twinkling. Then she looked dead at me and said, "I am a huge fan."

I turned to John a couple of times, assuming she was talking to him. And she said, "You." I wasn't exactly sure who she thought I was. Amy Irving is always a possibility. And recently I had been plucked out of line and ensconced at a prime table at a restaurant in Beverly Hills before I realized the reason I hadn't had to wait was that the maître d' (new to this country and obviously nearsighted) thought he was seating Julianne Moore. I had no idea who Ms. Taylor thought I was. I immediately responded, in all seriousness, "Oh, no, I'm not who you think I am. My name is Amy. I'm here with John."

She dismissed my denial as if I had made a hilarious joke. She persisted, taking my hand in both of hers and telling me that every day at four o'clock she gets a massage, and her masseuse knows to put on the USA Network so they can watch *Wings* repeats. She knew my character's name; she referenced a couple of plotlines. Surreal does not begin to describe that moment. Whether or not her effusive compliments were related to her having recently had brain surgery, we may never know.

Roddy McDowell came over and began to introduce

The Ritters:
Tex, Dorothy,
Tom, and John

My showbiz debut on
the box of the Easy-Bake
Oven, 1969 [*Art by the King
of Pop, Nelson De La Nuez*]

High school
graduation, 1980—
Amy with Mom
and Dad

*W*ith Mel Brooks on the set of *Robin Hood: Men in Tights*, 1992

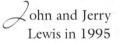

*J*ohn and Jerry Lewis in 1995

A Polaroid John sent from the set of *Sling Blade* (Pineapple Boy), 1995

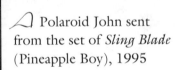

*V*enice, 1996

Backstage at World's
Greatest Magic, July 1998

Three's Company,
September 11, 1998

October 1998
[*Photo by Pam Springsteen*]

Stella Dorothy Ritter

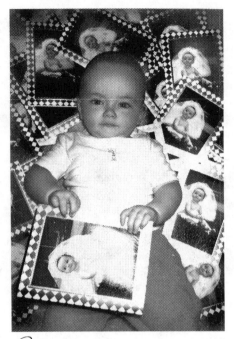

$\mathcal{S}$tella "helping us" mail
wedding invitations

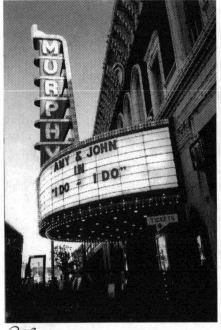

$\mathcal{M}$arquee of the Murphy
Theater the day of our wedding

$\mathcal{S}$eptember 18, 1999

$\mathcal{S}$tella, John, and Uncle Tommy
at a Dodgers game, 1999

*J*ohn reading *Caps for Sale* to Stella, summer 2000

*S*tella and John, August 2000

*S*tella at Strawberry Fields in Central Park, 2000

*S*tella and John in the Big Apple

*G*earing up to parasail
in Florida, January 2002

*J*ohn, Stella, and me, May 2002

Hawaii,
July 2002

With Clifford in our
backyard, summer 2002

People's Choice
Awards, 2003

Stella and John in Hawaii, July 2003

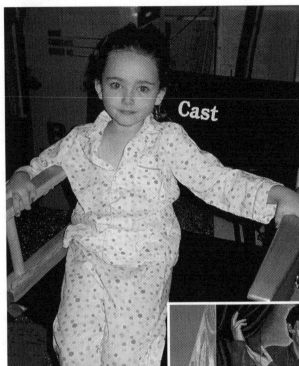

$\mathcal{S}$tella in her pjs at
8 Simple Rules,
August 2003

$\mathcal{W}$ith Jimmy Kimmel,
who was the driving
force behind the
Hollywood High mural,
July 2008

us to her. He was as surprised as I was when she recounted the whole thing to him. After a pause, he said, "Okay . . . and this is John Ritter." And she said, "Yes, yes, of course," then thanked us for coming, told us what was for brunch, and floated away. Okay, she didn't float, but she may as well have.

Honest to God, the most thrilling part of the entire day was the look on John's face. He was always wildly enthusiastic and encouraging about my career. Way more gung-ho about it than I ever was. This was just so cool for him. I got a little taste of what it must've been like for the kids to have had John for a father. He could not stop grinning. He was truly happy for me.

We filled our plates with some of the most seriously brunchy brunch food I had ever seen and made our way back to the living room. We saw Elizabeth (ooooh, first name basis) sitting in a chair across from Johnny Depp. They had plates of food in their laps and were engaged in a discussion about the headscarf he was wearing. He explained that he was in the midst of filming Hunter S. Thompson's *Fear and Loathing in Las Vegas* and that Hunter himself had given him a haircut.

John and I both stopped about ten feet away. Clearly we were not in the inner circle, but she was so damn gracious that we didn't know where to sit or what was appropriate. Just then, she bent down and patted the floor next to her. Relieved, John and I dutifully scrambled to her side and plopped down on the floor with our plates in our laps. At which point, two white, gorgeously groomed and evidently miffed Maltese dogs ran up to her chair. Elizabeth smiled at Johnny Depp and then at us. Apparently, we had misread her signal and had stolen the dogs' prized spot. They never stopped glaring at us the entire time we sat next to her. I felt like the gloating sibling who yells "shotgun" on the way to the station wagon, and then has to endure the glares from the backseat for the rest of the ride. Worth it.

chapter 12

A Broad

In the summer of 1996, Henry Winkler was to be honored at the first annual television festival in Nice, and he invited John and me to join him, his wife, Stacy, and their kids, and Marlee Matlin and her family for the event. John decided he wanted to make an extended vacation of it. We made plans to go to Venice and Florence before meeting the Winkler gang in France.

We were very excited for the trip. Neither one of us had ever been to Italy.

John bought every guidebook known to tourists, and I nearly started a fire in my brain trying to frantically rub together the creaky band of neurons that occasionally fired at the mention of art history. I knew just enough about the subject from Ms. Burton's art appreciation class in high school and my own hit or miss, pre-Google, mostly PBS-based "research" to get myself in trouble. Like knowing just a little bit of a foreign language: educating yourself haphaz-ardly on a subject, sincere as you may be, is a surefire way to get called out as a bullshitter. Somebody who really knows their stuff always seems to be lurking close enough to over-hear that one half-assed reference or telling mispronun-ciation that red-flags you. I'm always one dubious raised eyebrow away from humiliation.

The plane ride was an extended version of previous plane rides with John. He read twenty books, three news-papers, and a *Mad* magazine and then fell into a deep, loud sleep for the rest of the flight. I flew wide awake and hyper-aware for sixteen hours, cramming names of artists and their works into my head. The flight to Italy was surprisingly simi-lar to labor now that I can look back "fondly" on both. The minutes seemed like hours, my lower back was on fire, and I harbored a mild resentment that John was able to sleep through most of it. (Epidurals would not be an altogether bad idea for international flights.)

As we began our descent, even our first glimpse of Venice from the air was romantic. However, going through security was a little more "romantic" than I had bargained for. The contraband-sniffing guard dog kind of fell in love with me, so I was taken to the side and patted down . . . and up . . . and down . . . by a Venetian policeman. John never let me forget that I wasn't there ten minutes before I was felt up by an Italian guy. That's amore.

The boat ride to the Cipriani hotel was, honest to God, magical. We passed the island of Murano, world famous for its glass foundries, moved there centuries ago for fear their furnaces would ignite the mostly wooden buildings of

Venice. On the boat, the surreal quality of this trip started to catch up with us. We had the sense that we were on a journey no less magical than being taken up into a twister and plopped down in Oz.

The hotel was gorgeous and a little intimidating. It was the middle of the day and we were exhausted. The very well-meaning bellman was trying to explain the amenities in our room. We had no idea what he was talking about, so John tipped him and ushered him out the door as politely as he could.

We closed the blinds and fell into our bed. I pushed what I assumed was the light switch. There was a really loud mechanical noise from the foot of the bed as a gigantic box rose up, like the monolith from *2001: A Space Odyssey*. John reached over me and started pushing the button over and over, as the thing went up and down a couple times before grinding to a screeching stop halfway. We realized we had just broken the groovy ultramodern television. In 1996, this popping-up TV idea was new to us. We saw plenty of them in the years after that, but they were never that loud. At first, John resisted my suggestion that we had to call the front desk and confess. I convinced him that I couldn't sleep if we didn't. (Catholic.)

John picked up the phone on the nightstand to call the front desk, but I was so embarrassed that we had been there only minutes and had already done major damage to their hotel that I told him to use the phone in the bathroom so I could hide under the covers. I'm quite a chicken when it comes to confrontation and I did not want to hear the conversation in case it got sticky. He walked into the bathroom and after a moment called out to me that now the phone was broken, too. He sounded very frustrated. I could hear him saying, "Hello? Hello?! Front desk? . . . Dammit. Hello?!"

I tiptoed in there and saw him talking into the wall-mounted hair dryer. On purpose, of course. We sat on the bathroom floor and laughed our heads off; it was the perfect way for him to get his point across. I needed to let go a little. Neither one of us had ever invested any energy in trying to be cool. We were two dorks far away from home, and if the foreign environment fought us a little, so what? It's all about the adventure.

The next morning the manager of the hotel called to tell us that he had arranged a tour for us of the Murano glass factory and showroom. We didn't really have a game plan for the first day and we decided to go with the flow. A little boat arrived for us. We were very impressed by the Italian hospitality.

After a brief but very romantic cruise for two, we arrived at the island of Murano. We were met at the boat and escorted to the workshop, where we marveled at the glassblowers—craftsmen whose families had been perfecting and improving their art for centuries. The tour guide encouraged us to walk around the labyrinthine showroom. It had obviously been designed to impress, disorient, and impoverish. Every room was lined with showcases filled with gorgeous, pricey pieces, and eager salespeople hovered close by to assess our interest before leading us to another, pricier room.

At some point, John and I got separated for about ten

minutes. When I finally caught up with him, he was admir-
ing a beautiful jeweled glass wine decanter with four gob-
lets, each depicting one of the four seasons. I came around
the corner just in time to hear the salesman say that it was
$90,000. John looked trapped. He held up one goblet and
said, "How much for winter?" The guy was furious and dis-
gusted that we would think we could break up the set. I
pulled John into the corner of the room and we pretended
to argue. We whispered a little too loudly and recklessly,
waving our arms around a bit. This, it turns out, is a very
effective way to get escorted out of a Venetian glass showroom.

On our way back to town, John reminded me of the big
promise I had made back home. I had been a vegetarian for
fifteen years at that point. I didn't even eat cheese, except if
it was made with vegetable rennet—don't ask; believe me
you don't want to know. It's fairly doable in Los Angeles,
where inquiries to your waiter/actor about the rennet in
your lunch are often met with, "Dude, you're a vegetarian?
Aaaawesome!"

In Italy, however, John was worried that, for fear that I
would accidentally insult someone by questioning the content of their cheese, I would opt to just not eat. So I promised I would temporarily suspend the superstrict vegetarian
thing just while we were there. Cut to two years later: 1998,
me pregnant with Stella, ordering cheese with a side of
cheese—"Would you like Parmesan with that?" "You bet my
ass I do—and leave the grater."

The rest of our time in Venice was like a dream. No one
seemed to recognize John and he loved it. It was always

fun for me to see his sweet face out in the world, without his requisite baseball cap and sunglasses. When I would detect an American accent in the crowd, I'd whistle the banjo theme from *Deliverance* and he would whip them back on. He loved his fans and was always gracious when he was recognized. We just didn't want to change gears from romantic vacation mode to fan mode, by getting into a ten-minute conversation about "Who was hotter, Janet or Chrissy?"

We traveled the canals in gondolas, feasted in trattorias, and huddled in cavernous cathedrals, lighting candles, making promises, and whispering about our future together. On our last day there, we stood in the middle of St. Mark's Square. It was filled with laughter and color and music and people and pigeons. We were on a kind of ecstatic sensory overload. The place was electrifying and romantic and I was desperate to capture that feeling and keep it in my heart. I put my head down on John's chest and said, "It's too much. I'll never remember all of this." He lifted up my chin and turned me around slowly by my shoulders, giving me a 360-degree view of the plaza, until I was face-to-face with him again. He said, "You'll remember this forever."

At the train station, as John struggled to get our bags out of the boat, I wandered away. I was absolutely mesmerized by this beautiful statue of Mary that had been there for hundreds and hundreds of years. She was strewn with flowers, tributes to her from travelers, just like those left by sailors years ago. There was a lengthy inscription in Latin at the base of the statue. What jumped out at me was that she was called Stella Maris. The Star of the Sea. The North Star that guided the ancient mariners.

I rushed back to John, who was still juggling our luggage, and told him that if we ever had a baby girl we should name her Stella. He was real quiet for a minute, blinked a couple of times, bit his lower lip, and then said, "Did you swipe a gondola? What the hell is in your suitcase?"

I took my bag and rolled it. I pouted imperceptibly (my specialty) the forty yards or so to our train. This was a definite reoccurring theme in my life: this getting-overexcited-and-assuming-the-person-I'm-talking-to-will-feel-the-same-way-I-do thing. Burns every time. But as we were standing on the steps of the train ready to board, John leaned in very close to my ear. He whispered, "Like Brando . . . like *Streetcar* . . . Stella . . . I love it."

We always talked about going back and would sort of melt into each other any time we would see an image of Venice. After Stella was born, he would say, "When she's six, right? Six seems like the right age for our journey back with Stella."

In our living room is a cabinet with "treasures" from our travels. Stella and I recently opened it for the first time in a long time. I showed her a golf-ball-size piece of clear glass with a tiny goldfish inside. John and I had seen hundreds of them in Venice. We bought one whose eyes didn't quite match because he looked like he needed us. Charlie Brown's Christmas tree theory. They cost about three dollars in American money, but Stella admired it like it was worth $90,000. She asked if we could go to Venice some day.

Yikes. Can we? Without John? These are the kind of things I'm still working out. Is Venice even still there? It's one of those innocently arrogant feelings that accompany romantic love: This is our place; it exists for us alone.

The train to Florence was packed. John and I gave our seats to an old couple from America who were standing right next to us in the aisle. We sat, instead, on the floor and could barely see out the window. The fields of sunflowers blooming along the way were blurred by the speed of our train. It was like an impressionistic segue to our next adventure.

Our hotel was just outside the city and we walked everywhere. The first night we decided to take a cab to dinner from our hotel. When the driver asked us, in broken English, where we wanted to go, John said, "Florence." Well, technically we were already in Florence, so the guy just stared at us. A very awkward tourist moment passed. Then I piped up with: "Town . . . Florence town."

As the driver pulled into traffic, John started singing, softly at first, "Won't you take me to . . . FLORENCE TOWN" to the tune of "Funky Town." He kept it up for the whole drive. I joined in about halfway there. By the time we got to the city we were singing at "performance level" and had added backseat *Solid Gold*–style dance moves. John, who was never afraid to be a goofball, clearly loved Italy and the sense of freedom that his anonymity afforded him. When we got to the city, John took some lira out of his pocket and asked, "How much do we owe you?"

The driver pointed to him and said, *"Tre Cuori in Affitto."* We sat there, looking down at our Italian money, not quite sure what he meant. The guy shook his head disappointedly and took a few bills out of John's hand. We got out of the taxi, and as the guy pulled off, he yelled out his window in our direction, *"Tre Cuori in Affitto!"*

The next day the line for the Uffizi art museum was about two blocks long. I had to get in there and see Botticelli's *Birth of Venus,* or as Ms. Burton referred to it: "Venus on the half-shell." I always loved that painting and it was my inspiration for the tame but definitely nude linoleum print I displayed for my high school senior art show. I eventually took it down under pressure from the principal and various helpful nuns.

We were told that the wait to get into the museum would be about an hour. It was a hot, bright day in Florence, and we stood in line, our hats the only source of shade. We decided that the cooler alternative would be for us to each walk around by ourselves for half an hour while the other kept our place in line. John struck out on his own first. I had practically melted into the sidewalk by the time he sauntered back a full hour later with a box of cigars and got in front of me in line.

When I asked him what took him so long, he turned around, smiled, whipped off his hat and said, "I got a haircut!" The block-long line, all behind us now, murmured, and then came the first *"Tre Cuori in Affitto!"* It was followed by about a dozen more, all in different tones and with a lot of pointing. The museum guard (yes, we had made it to the door) told us that *Tre Cuori in Affitto* was Italian for *Three Hearts for Rent,* the name of *Three's Company* in Italy.

John had no idea that the show had been dubbed in Italian and aired on television there. We guessed that the people in Venice had been too in love to notice. So he signed some autographs and took some pictures and saw the *Birth of Venus* through his requisite sunglasses. It didn't matter; we had a ball in Florence. Between John's guidebooks and my spotty knowledge of Italian art we managed to laugh and sing and dance and eat and marvel our way through one of the most beautiful cities on earth.

After three days in Florence, we flew to the South of France, where the mayor of Nice would be giving Henry Winkler the key to the city to kick off their Cannes-style television festival. We stayed at the Hotel Negresco with Henry and the other honorees. The first day, everyone gathered in the lobby to be driven to the festival. There was a crowd of fans and press outside, who had heard that Henry was in there. They started calling for him to come out. He obliged and walked through the front doors and stood at the top of the steps. The crowd got really excited and began chanting his name. "Henri! Henri! Henri!"

Henry was so sweet. When he waved to the crowd, the chanting escalated to *Evita* level. John and I were sitting in the lobby, kind of watching this love-fest from the wings. Then Henry walked back in toward us, grabbed John by the elbow, and pulled him to the door. John protested at first, and then reluctantly went along with him.

When the crowd saw John they looked confused, slowly quieted down, then one guy yelled in a heavy French accent, "What's your name?" Henry opened his mouth to speak, but John cut him off, yelling, "Jeff!" A couple of them tried to start a "Jeff" chant, figuring he was somebody they were supposed to recognize. There we were at the First Annual International Television Festival and nobody had a clue who John was. Anyone who knew him could tell you that this is the kind of thing he lived for. He turned a potentially humiliating situation into an opportunity to launch into an extended public improvisation that seemed to be loosely based on "The Emperor's New Clothes." The fact that the whole bit hinged on John being completely unrecognized solidified my perception of him as the rarest of the rare: an ego-free actor. He loved the acting and playing much more than he ever loved the notoriety.

Later when we were at the actual event, a French reporter recognized him (Jeff) from the steps of the Negresco and asked him for an interview. John regaled him with stories and anecdotes about his famous American show, *Hello, Jeff*. He invented plots and characters out of thin air. More reporters gathered around and scribbled down everything John said, sometimes with the aid of an interpreter. One of them asked him what his favorite episode was. He paused reflectively and said it would have to be the final episode of the series, the highly rated "Goodbye, Hello, Jeff."

Over the next few days people would occasionally greet him with "Hello, Jeff," then laugh knowingly because they had inadvertently said the title of his "famous American show." If one of their buddies innocently asked them who John was, they would shoot back the French equivalent of "*Jeff*! You idiot." John wondered, though, why no one ever asked him his last name. I told him they probably thought he didn't need one anymore. "You know: Cher, Elvis, and Jeff."

chapter you know what *

---

*Actors are notoriously superstitious. No whistling in the theater. Always leave a light on onstage. Never utter the name of "the Scottish play." John and I and every actor who has spent anytime onstage are made well aware of these old standards early on. But John had a little something extra to deal with. A full-blown lifelong case of *triskaidekaphobia*: fear of the number thirteen. So in honor of John: no apterchay irteenthay.

chapter 14

Stella

After *Wings* ended, I shot the pilot episode for the WB sitcom *Alright Already*. Carol Leifer was the executive producer, writer, and star of the show, and she and I became fast friends. Carol had gone from the world of stand-up comedy to writing for *Seinfeld* and dozens of other super-high-profile television shows. She was hilarious on *Alright Already,* and I felt lucky to be cast as her best friend, Renee. If you're gonna play the second banana, this show was the place to do it.

Carol had recently gone through a life-changing—make that *life-affirming*—breast cancer scare. It turned out to be a false alarm. One of the best things about Carol is that once her consciousness is raised about something, she becomes a tenacious advocate. It was January 1998, and we had been working together for a few months. She knew I was thirty-five at the time and she urged—make that *lovingly pestered*—

me to make an appointment for my first mammogram, even calling me on our day off to make sure I had followed through. I assured her that I had. (I hadn't.) Lying about a mammogram seemed like more than bad manners; it seemed like bad luck. As much as I pooh-pooh other people's quirky superstitions, I tend to obey mine. Neurotic or just half-Irish, you be the judge.

To counteract the feeling that I had just induced cancer, I called to make an appointment. When the very polite receptionist taking my information got to the part of the form that asked me for the date of my last period, I was stumped. As I always am. My cycle is regular but my monthly organizational skills are anything but. I never write it down, although I grew up with a sister who, at my mother's urging, wrote "Me Due" at twenty-eight-day intervals on all of her calendars. To jog my memory, I always have to think back and pin my start date to some event. This time it was Thanksgiving, so I answered, "Six weeks ago." There was a pause so pregnant you could drive a baby buggy through it, followed by the receptionist's drawn out "o-o-o-k-a-a-a-y . . ." and then I heard myself say, "Holy shit."

John and I were over the moon. We decided that I shouldn't tell anyone at work. I didn't know if the WB was going to pick up our series for a second season. If it did get renewed, I would tell Carol then. (It didn't, but she was thrilled for me when I finally told her that I was expecting.) The only one at *Alright Already* who knew my little secret was my longtime friend, stand-in, and partner in crime, Cheryl Henry. Ever since we first met on the set of *Matlock* in 1990, she had been at my side through thick and thin. In this case, I was getting thicker by the minute. Most women suffer through a couple months of morning sickness. My first trimester was comprised of afternoon, evening, and all-night sickness. This left about an hour window in the morning for chow time. It was the only time of day that I was not flat-out queasy. And I did not waste one minute of it. I would strap on the old feedbag the minute I hit the set. And Cheryl, God love her, followed me around with a plate of food all day, the movable feast providing a convenient explanation for busting out of my wardrobe.

During the last month of the show, I got a commercial job for the part of the *Oh Thank Heaven for 7-Eleven* angel, including a few television ads and radio spots. Between the first fitting for my angel costume and the actual shoot a few weeks later, I had gained a very noticeable ten pounds. I ended up shooting the commercials with the back of my flowing white gown unzipped to allow for my undeniable tummy. The first day of the shoot, I was in my trailer between takes, rubbing my swollen feet, while my cumbersome angel wings hung, dejected, on the wardrobe rack. The phone rang and it was John and his daughter Carly on the line. We had promised that she would be the first to know when we found out the sex of the baby, and we had just gotten the verdict that morning.

I chatted with her casually, describing my ludicrous getup and recounting the morning's wardrobe debacle. Then I said, as nonchalantly as I could, "Oh, by the way, Carly, I've got something for you. You've never had one before and I'm pretty sure you're gonna love it."

She asked me, "What is it?"

I said, "A sister."

The sound that came out of her was somewhere between a yelp and a squeal. Genuine joy. In the background, I could hear John laughing his goofy, too loud, so-into-the-moment-he-would-forget-where-he-was laugh. A laugh so familiar that I can still picture his face at that instant, even though I never actually saw it. The moment caught me off guard and I burst out crying. My laboriously applied mascara began to puddle and run. As if being a pregnant angel wasn't bizarre enough, my eyes had now taken on a decidedly Goth look that was probably a bit more "angel of death" than the 7-Eleven execs had in mind. I washed, rinsed, and reapplied. (The actress version of *pick yourself up, dust yourself off, start all over again.*) The commercial must go on.

Now that we knew that our little belly bean was a girl for sure, we needed to start calling her by name. Stella. That was the name we kept coming back to: There was the mariners' statue of Mother Mary in Venice, known as Stella Maris. There was the jazz classic "Stella by Starlight." And there was Stella Adler, John's beloved acting teacher. Along with Mary Carver, John Blankenship, and Nina Foch, she was the backbone of John's theatrical education. It was no accident that John studied with her; she was a friend and mentor to John's all-time-favorite actor, Marlon Brando, who bellowed that famous line in *A Streetcar Named Desire,* "Stellaaaahhh!" So Stella it was.

Even though my burgeoning belly was making it nearly impossible to shoot anything out of order, I snagged a part in the TV movie *Last Man on the List* that was shooting in Toronto that spring. The movie starred Nicolette Sheridan and a fella named John Ritter. "Aha! Another casting mystery solved." (That's what my friend Peter says when you find there's been nepotism at play. If you ever notice a perplexing choice of actor for a role, wait for the credits. All will be revealed.)

John and I had a ball in Toronto. Billy Bob Thornton was there at the same time shooting *Pushing Tin* with John Cusack and Angelina Jolie. The Rolling Stones were also in town and John and I, having seen them together in Dallas when we first met, were dying to go to the concert. Angelina was very good friends with Mick Jagger and had starred in the Stones' music video for "Anybody Seen My Baby." She offered to take us backstage and introduce us to the band. I went all out and wore a sad, stretchy-wetchy, leopard-print maternity pantsuit for the occasion, and wedged my Fred Flintstone feet into a pair of precarious high-heels. Pretty. Not only was I meeting Mick at four months gone, but I was doing it while standing next to freakin' Angelina Jolie. Never knew it was possible to feel so gigantic and so invisible at the same time.

It was a thrill just the same. As we watched the show from the audience, I noticed something strange happening. Natural, but strange to me—Stella was kicking for the first time. And kicking. And kicking. John stood behind me with his hands on my Lycra leopard-print tummy and swayed with both of us to "Satisfaction." He was a happy, happy boy.

At seven months, I got to the point in my pregnancy where I could no longer comfortably play my guitar (or breathe or wear shoes, for that matter). I wanted to strum songs for Stella with the chords resonating in the amniotic fluid. I guess I was shooting for a "singing in the shower" effect. I started writing a lullaby, "Stella-Bella," but my burgeoning belly kept pushing my guitar farther and farther away from me every day. My arms weren't getting any longer, so it became incrementally more awkward to play.

The piano was not an option. The four lessons I had struggled through in fourth grade were still seared in my memory. Scarring not just for me; Sister Cecelia had seemed as relieved as I was when I told her I wanted to quit. Now, with my ergonomic instrument choices limited, I opted to buy a harmonica.

In July, I went to Wilmington, North Carolina, to join John while he was shooting *Holy Joe,* a beautiful movie about miracles. John played Reverend Joe Cass, an Episcopal priest who is experiencing a crisis of faith. Joe, who is also a volunteer fireman, saves a young man named Ezekiel during a miraculous rescue, aided by an unknown fireman, who Ezekiel claims to be Jesus. Joe doesn't believe it, but appreciates the packed pews that the headline-making controversy generates. He begins to ponder the everyday miracles in his own life and decides to leave room for the possibility that the rescue miracle was real.

John loved the script and couldn't wait to start filming the movie. I joined him a few days into the shoot, arriving in the middle of a heat wave, the likes of which I had never experienced. I foolishly thought I had some expertise in the area of humidity, having grown up in the Ohio River basin, affectionately known as "Sinus Valley." Forget Walmart; in Cincinnati, the folks are praying for a megachain of Sudaphed-R-Us stores to move in. The humidity in North Carolina was humbling and the heat nearly melted me.

On a walk into town from our cute little hotel, I almost bit it. I was advised to stay indoors, but there were some fish and chips calling my name. I had just recently lifted the ban on eating fish and chicken that I had imposed on myself at nineteen. John had taken me to a place the night before where I had eaten everything but the plate. I honestly could not get the fish and chips out of my head. I dreamed about them all night. I would have had to put tartar sauce on my unlaced Nikes if I couldn't get to them. They were beckoning me from about ten blocks away and I was determined to make them mine. I brought a Payday candy bar to sustain me on my quest.

I was about a block and a half down the road when I started feeling fizzy. People were looking at me funny. I remember listing to the left and kind of bouncing off a couple of storefronts before I came to rest, flat-faced and sweaty, against a restaurant window. I'm sure the oversize, hyperventilating Garfield stuck to the glass was a charming site for the diners inside. The owner brought me in, sat me down, and draped a wet towel around my neck. I must've been doing some delirious heatstroke babbling because the next thing I knew there was a plate of fish and chips in front of me. Not a mirage, the real thing. Apparently, in Wilmington, North Carolina, there is no shortage of hospitality or fried fish. I chowed down and then was escorted by a chatty busboy back to the hotel, where I fell sound asleep for five hours.

By the time I woke up, the movie had wrapped for the day and John was back. I was going to tell him about my crazy day, when I noticed the look on his face. Not good. He told me that he nearly passed out shooting the fire rescue scene. John had been suited up in all of his authentic firefighter gear, including oxygen, and when he came back down the ladder, the stunt coordinator could hardly believe the amount of air John had used up. He told John that he needed to breathe more slowly and to try to ignore the heat and the adrenaline. The temperature was 110°F that day, and John was in full firefighter regalia, climbing a ladder toward a manufactured but nonetheless roaring inferno. I commiserated by telling him about my ill-fated adventure, staggering through the streets like Otis the drunk from Mayberry RFD.

We talked about breathing. About breath. I went into my suitcase and broke out my harmonica. We breathed into it. We were just two people who needed a little reminding that inhaling and exhaling, although involuntary, sometimes needed to be infused with a modicum of intention.

John fumbled around with some notes until "Red River Valley" started to pour out of him. He had learned how to play the song for a scene with Lucille Ball on her last sitcom. Thus is the continuing education of the actor. He asked me if I knew the words. That was definitely something he appreciated about me—I almost always know the words. He played, I sang. Years later, after John died, I found my harmonica in his stuff. He had laid claim to it. I tried to figure out how to play "Red River Valley," but I couldn't get through it. I was singing the lyrics in my head.

Stella

From this valley, they say you are going,
We will miss your bright eyes and sweet smile.
For they say you are taking the sunshine
That has brightened our pathways awhile.

On the Fourth of July, the cast and crew had the day off. John and I had spent the entire day ordering in, watching TV, and luxuriating in our tiny but thankfully air-conditioned hotel room. When night rolled around, we sat on the porch swing in the dark. The fireworks boomed overhead, their smoky trails clung to the sky. Stella twisted and kicked along with the show. Maybe it had reminded her of the Rolling Stones concert.

After the last climactic bursts of the display, she stopped and seemed to listen to the silence along with the rest of the town. Then a huge lightning bolt lit up the sky. The kind I remember from my childhood that would seem to turn night into day for an instant. A pounding rainstorm rolled in on the heels of a nerve-shattering thunderclap. At the sound, Stella seemed to stretch out all four of her limbs in an attempt to perform an intrauterine cartwheel. Impossible, sure, but when you're pregnant you develop a whole fantasy about your baby's acrobatic life inside you. The world your baby inhabits isn't solely in your womb; they dwell in your imagination at the same time. That night, in my mind, Stella wanted out. Right then and there. I was claustrophobic for her. The fireworks, the thunderstorm, the humidity, and the second helping of fish and chips (yes, I was still at it) had conspired to send me into a silent panic attack.

Ever true to form, John offered to "relax" me. All through my pregnancy and even in those last couple of months, when every romantic endeavor was decidedly more *sumo* than *porno,* John remained unfailingly ardent. When I would point out my laughable condition and ever-distorting silhouette, he would always counter with a hearty, "That don't make me no never mind." And he meant it.

This go-around we were halfway out on the porch, sheltered under the roof of the veranda. Every once in a while the wind would shift direction and we would get rained on for a few seconds, like we were in some high-tech produce section of the supermarket. It actually worked beautifully to calm all of us. John would always refer to it as the first night he rocked Stella to sleep.

chapter 15

Ssstteeelllaaahhh!

At eight months along, I found myself once again on a plane. I was on my way to join John at Caesar's Palace in Las Vegas. He was there to film the fifth installment of the television special *The World's Greatest Magic.* Rouged up and in full host mode, Sir Tux-a-lot (as I liked to refer to his master of ceremonies incarnation) would be introducing some of the most ingenious magic acts from around the world.

I had accompanied him on the weekend-long shoot for the two preceding years, where they had put us up in a beautiful room with lots and lots of little goodies—the works. This go-around, John had checked in the day prior to my arrival and had coyly refused to describe our hotel room to me on the phone. I was understandably psyched to get there and see for myself what Caesar's Palace had in store for us this time.

When the bellman opened the door, I was gob smacked. Judging by the size of our hotel room, *World's Greatest Magic IV* must have been a hit; they seemed to have ratcheted up the production budget quite a bit. The suite was over the top. As *Ohio-shy* as I was about the opulent decor, I was overjoyed by the sheer size of the place. "Mommy-to-be" needed some room to stretch out. I was, after all, still in the process of making peace with my new figure. I was in denial about how large I had grown over the previous month. My dysmorphia had landed me in a couple of pickles . . . which I promptly ate. I kid. I had recently found myself inextricably wedged in a ladies room stall (damn you, inward opening door) and inadvertently clearing off a restaurant tabletop with my rogue belly (damn you, unintentional Oliver Hardy comedy bits).

I was overjoyed to be situated in my roomy, size-appropriate suite. California king–size bed, sunken whirlpool bathtub, crazy awesome oversize basket of Pepperidge Farm Mint Milano Cookies: a pregnant lady's dream. Munching away, as I giddily scoped out our large and lovely weekend digs, my eyes drifted upward, where I saw *it:* a huge round mirror affixed to the ceiling. This feature seemed more than out of place in the buffet capital of the world, it seemed downright cruel. I had lived the previous twenty years of my life as a fairly strict vegetarian. Now, conveniently throwing the "eating for two" card, I had taken the lid off my usual dietary restrictions, as well as every pint of Ben & Jerry's I could get my hands on. The fifty or so pounds I had put on during my pregnancy weren't so much due to my being "with child" as they were about being "with Chunky Monkey."

Romance-wise, I was more than just a *good sport* during my pregnancy. Happy hormones were in overdrive; I could not leave the poor guy alone. John obliged every time I tapped his shoulder to go a few rounds, bless his heart. A former bantamweight, I was now a formidable contender. Possibly out of the same defense mechanism employed by frightened cats and puffer fish, John bulked up by a few pounds himself during my last trimester. Even though the "mirror over the bed" thing is never good—never—we were undeterred. There should have been a card on the nightstand stating, *Warning: Objects in mirror are shockingly identical to how they appear; you will never be able to un-see this.*

I was a happy, huge camper for that surprisingly romantic weekend. I broke out the ole stretch leopard-print maternity pantsuit. The same lame/fabulous outfit that I had rocked backstage with Mick was now gracing the wings of the main stage at Caesar's. For Vegas, my getup was understated, classy even. As John and I goofed around between acts, overly spangled, easily mesmerized magician's assistants from the four corners of the earth hovered around me, as if my pregnancy were an ingenious new illusion.

During our Vegas weekend, I had fully surrendered to the accelerated blooming and blossoming that was blowing my mind (and figure) a little bit more each day. Every morning brought the feeling that a new part of me was pregnant. I had months before discovered my feet were expecting (twins, no less!). I was now in the home stretch (mark). Knees, knuckles, and elbows disappeared. Even my pierced earrings didn't fit.

On the flight home to L.A., I blew my nose and it deployed like a lifejacket. All I wanted to do was go back home and get in our pool. And that is exactly what I did. Once home, I drifted, body and mind buoyed by an overburdened pink plastic pool float, tripping on the fact that Stella was simultaneously floating inside me. Human nesting dolls . . . ah . . . peace. The cannonball that John executed two feet away from my head was upsetting only for my inflatable craft. My blissed-out state of mind was impervious to party crashers.

When I surfaced, I saw that John was wincing in pain. He said that he had stepped on a rock or something when he had jumped in. I could tell he was hopping around on one foot even though we were both emerged up to our armpits. Limber as ever, he turned his head and hoisted his left foot above the water for my inspection. He said, "I can't look, is it bad?"

It was, in fact, the opposite of bad. There, proudly adorning his gnarly pinky toe, was a sparkling diamond and sapphire engagement ring (not a moment too soon). After a brief but brilliant engagement-ring-stuck-on-a-toe bit, he took it off, held it out to me, and asked, "Will you marry me, Stella's mama?" I replied that I had always imagined he'd be kneeling when he finally popped the question. Sure enough, with faux consternation, he slowly sunk and then pantomimed an elaborate underwater marriage proposal to my belly. I accepted by signaling "okay" with my submerged left hand. He slipped the ring on my finger then shot to the surface gasping for breath and grinning from ear to ear. We were taking the plunge.

The night of September 10, we were on the couch enjoying the MTV Music Video Awards, waiting for our beloved A.F.K.A. Prince to make his appearance and rock our world. I told John that I was kind of having crampy feelings and I wondered aloud if this was *it*. He said to relax and that he would let me know when I was in labor. Deferring to his experience with this kind of thing, I chalked up my discomfort to the mushroom pot stickers he had talked me into at dinner.

During a commercial break, he walked out of the room to track down that damn elusive pack of Tums that only seemed to be handy when I didn't need it. The show came back on and they introduced Prince. John, now tenaciously rooting around in my purse after fruitlessly performing a full-on kitchen grid search, heard the music and shouted, "Is it on? . . . Huh? . . . Is it on?" Receiving no response, he walked into the TV room to find me kneeling on the floor, facedown on the seat cushion. He later told me that I looked like the little girl who'd fallen asleep saying her prayers. Oh, I was saying my prayers all right, but this little girl was wide awake. He walked up behind the couch, leaned over, and said, "Okay, Amy, *now* you're in labor." Ya think? Thank you, Midwife John, I'll take it from here.

When we got to the hospital, my contractions were five minutes apart but I was barely dilated. Ten hours later, well into the next day—same story. This fact, unlike the hospital pillow I was fiercely clenching, was hard for me to grasp. Recognizing that they had a "visual learner" on their hands, the staff employed a dilation chart. It was a notebook-size plastic template with ten different size holes to denote widening cervical dimensions. Years before, I had lost a similar contraption while relocating from New York to Los Angeles. Mine was a gadget intended to assist the clueless cook with estimating appropriate noodle portions. Some enterprising passerby must have found my pasta measure along the roadside and decided, "I'm going to repurpose this son of a gun and sell them to obstetricians." Now Nurse Nora was holding it in front of my face to help me visualize the goal. With horror, I realized that my body was stalled at *pasta for one* and I wasn't allowed to push until it was *Sunday dinner at the Corleones'*. John suggested that we might want to rethink my natural childbirth plan.

First, I wanted to attempt the age-old method of employing gravity by getting up and walking around a little bit. John steadied me as I shuffled my way down the hall. We had barely passed a waiting room brimming with expectant fathers, when the familiar rumble of recognition began to roil. This disparate gathering of men had nothing in common besides the shared waiting game that their roles as expectant fathers required. Now, resolutely bonded by their love of all things *Three's Company,* they approached en masse for a closer look at Jack Tripper in the flesh.

Clearly, this labor-hastening strategy was not going to work. There's private, there's public, and then there's "WAAAAAHHHH, Jack! Dude! Where's Mr. Furley?!" Even Baby Stella knew enough not to emerge during a testosterone- and adrenaline-fueled high-five-a-thon. John demurred as gracefully as he could, nodding to them charmingly while whispering to me through a gritted smile, "Keep moving." He gracefully pivoted my big, awkward body and aimed me back down the hall from whence we came. Without him I would have been like a school bus negotiating a hairpin turn in a narrow cul-de-sac.

When we got back to our room, John closed the door behind us and clicked on the boom box we had brought from home. Preloaded, was Prince's *Graffiti Bridge,* track three, and we goofily danced to the appropriately titled "Release It." Not only was the name in keeping with the spirit of the moment, but the first line of the lyric happens to be: "Yo, Stella, if U think I'm afraid of U . . ." Our girl arrived in the late afternoon the next day. By then, DJ Daddy had changed up the mood a bit with a little Stevie Wonder. "Isn't she lovely?" Yep, she sure was.

The day after Stella was born, I turned thirty-six. It wasn't my birthday or anything; labor just hurt so bad that it aged me an entire year. Okay, it *was* my birthday—best one ever, in fact. I spent the day feeding my baby and calling my relatives. Most babies suck. But sometimes babies suck at sucking. Luckily, Stella had taken to nursing, right out of the gate.

Once home, however, the dynamic changed up a bit. The child would not go to sleep. She was colicky. Colicky. I had heard the term my entire life. Apparently, I, too, had been infamously colicky. My dad would tell stories of walking me around in his arms to quiet me. It worked only when I was held by my dad, and it worked only if he kept moving. After a dozen hours a day on his feet at his store, he would come home and relieve my mom. When I was older, he loved to demonstrate for me how he would try in vain to fake me out. Rocking hips back and forth as he slowly attempted to bend his knees and sit down, the minute his butt would hit the couch I would begin to wail. I was now paying the colic karmic price.

When Stella was about a week old, my sister Ann called to check in on her baby sister and her baby sister's baby. I told her that this was a very enlightening experience that made me absolutely sure that I would be a wonderful grandmother someday. "I love hanging out with Stella and taking care of her all day long. But every evening around 8:00 p.m. I find myself standing out on our front porch, waiting for her mother to come pick her up for the night." Not too far from the truth.

After a couple of weeks, it started to dawn on me that the only time Stella would actually fall asleep and stay asleep for longer than two hours was when we were soaking together in the bathtub. Sometimes just running our bath would be enough to calm her down. I finally realized that it was not so much the warm bath, but white noise created by the water flowing out of the faucet that was lulling Stella to sleep. After about a week of nonstop trickling, John brought me to my senses. He walked into the bathroom, turned off the faucet, and said, "Okay, you two, out of the tub. I'm sure we can re-create the same effect by rifling through our water bill for the month."

I burst out crying, which woke up Stella, who immediately joined in. John now had two sleep-deprived bawling babies on his hands. He looked like he was about to join the club. Then a giant smile flashed across his face and he clapped his hands together like he was having one of those old-fashioned "eureka" moments, and dashed out of the room. I could hear him digging around in his closet. He walked back in with a gadget that looked like a miniature spaceship. It was a white noise machine that Markie Post had given him for his dressing room when they starred together again in *Hearts Afire* back in 1994. We had messed with it at the time, sampling the creepy heartbeat setting, the crashing waves setting, the babbling brook . . . Oh dear God, the blessed babbling brook setting. He plugged the cord into the wall and blasted the babbling stream sound at maximum volume. Stella instantly stopped wailing, looked around a little, then let out a big sigh and nestled in for a snooze.

When I told Ann about our white noise revelation, she replied, "She gets that from you." According to her, when Dad wasn't at home to walk me to sleep, my mom would just turn on the vacuum and leave the room. It did the trick every time. Still does. I need to lie down and take a nap if I even think about vacuuming.

chapter 16

Do Us Part

"Don't forget your Mr. Mooneys."

We were packing for our wedding in Ohio. And I didn't want any mistakes. Early on in our relationship, I had begun to point out to John a simple fact he had somehow missed all his life. Whenever he was on *The Tonight Show* or any other talk shows, he always sat with his legs crossed ankle over knee. Inevitably, the pant leg on one side would ride up and expose a healthy bit of Ritter calf. Clearly, above sock/ below hem nudity does not pack the same punch as a nip slip, but it proves distracting nonetheless.

We would watch his talk show appearances together, anticipating, and eventually wagering on, when the flash of leg would occur. It was all fun and games until John went on *The Tonight Show* to promote *Sling Blade.* In the middle of his interview, John's focus seemed to be split. His mouth was talking about the movie, but the rest of him was all about the socks. We sat on the TV room couch and watched the broadcast in horror as the truth unfolded. Inadvertently, my overly fastidious fascination with his socks had induced in him what looked like a tic. As he was going on about filming in Arkansas, he began pulling up one sock and then the other, adjusting and readjusting. Overnight, he had developed OCD: obsessive calf disorder.

After his segment was over he began clicking around the dial to see what else was on. We landed on a *The Lucy Show* episode from the seventies. Lucy was outdoors—I believe she was up to some wacky hijinks (just a guess). Up rides her boss, Mr. Mooney, on a bicycle. He was sporting a pith helmet, hiking vest, Bermuda shorts, and really tall, black dress socks that ended right under his knees. John jumped up and pointed to the TV. "Amy, that's what I need. Mr. Mooney socks!" After that I always made sure he was well stocked . . . or socked.

Our wedding was to be no exception. It had been ten years since we had met. I was not about to let this man get cold feet, literally or otherwise. Equipped with half a dozen pairs of Mooneys and a tuxedo, John was fully prepared for the big day.

I, on the other hand, was not as "good to go." My best friend, Sissy Slayton, had basically done all the work. She was my matron of honor but, thankfully, she doubled as the full-on wedding planner. I had no idea what to do or how to do it. She organized everything. Printed the programs. Booked the reception. It wasn't just due to logistics; the fact that she lived in Cincinnati was just icing on the cake (the chocolate wedding cake with butter cream icing that *she* found). I am, hmm, how can I put this? Not a multitasker. I'm barely a tasker. I am more of an idea person.

Sissy has known this about me since high school. By our junior year in art class, we had developed a symbiotic art project relationship. I would surreptitiously redraw the faces and hands on projects she handed in. She did all the detail, design, and, thank God, the perspective on my projects. Not surprisingly, she has gone on to make quite a name for herself in the world of industrial design. But not before organizing a kick-ass wedding for me.

The only part I handled was the actual venue for the ceremony. Our wedding was to take place at the Murphy Theater in Wilmington, Ohio. The theater was built by my great-great-uncle, Charles Webb Murphy. He was the owner of the Chicago Cubs from 1906–08. Having made his fortune in the big city, he returned to his hometown of Wilmington to build what would become the centerpiece of the town. The theater hosted and boasted acts from all over the world, from vaudeville to classical music, and was also a movie house. I had no relatives left on the Murphy side of the family, so having our wedding at the theater was a way to honor my mother. I figured that John and Dorothy Yasbeck had romanced each other in the seats, Tex and Dorothy Ritter had romanced each other on the screen, and John and I would get married on the stage.

Our guests, coming mostly from Los Angeles and New York, would board a party bus that would be taking them on the forty-five-minute ride to Wilmington. Afterward, it would bring them back to Cincinnati for the reception. Sissy booked The Waterfront, an elegant docked riverboat restaurant and nightclub, where our reception was to be held.

A couple of days before the ceremony, John and Stella and I flew into town. I was as discombobulated as any bride-to-be with a one-year-old could be. We checked into the honeymoon suite downtown at the Cincinnatian Hotel. We baby-proofed the suite, as usual, using just the hotel room objects available, MomGyver style. Stella was a big-time cruiser. She had never crawled. But she had been monkey-walking around the house by pulling herself to her feet and hanging on for dear life to anything she could use to support herself. She hadn't walked yet, but it was in the offing. In anticipation, pillows were strapped to table corners and couch cushions arranged like pontoons on the floor around the bed. Probably the first time the honeymoon suite had looked this way *before* the wedding night.

The morning of the big day, we made a mad dash to the minimart around the corner with Stella in tow. We over-did it, as usual, and threw way, way, way too much stuff in the cart. It was obvious to me that I was overcompensating for the separation anxiety I felt welling up inside me. As ex-cited as I was about our big day (not a moment too soon, either, considering we had met ten years earlier, almost to the day . . . oh right, and we had a one-year-old, oops), the Stella factor was making me nervous as hell. Soon I would be in the car driving almost an hour away with Sissy and the Will to my Grace, Roger Stricker. Once I handed Stella over to my sisters, I would not be seeing her again for hours. I kid you not; this would be the longest I had ever been away from her. For one year and one week, Stella and I had been joined at the hip—make that *nip*. She was on an occasional bottle by then, so that wasn't exactly the problem.

On the bright side, the longer I went without nursing her, the better I looked in my bridal gown. It had a Marilyn Monroe–style halter top that I could've never filled out before my daughter, and never will again. Stella, I dedicate Bob Hope's theme song to you: "Thanks for the mammories."

I scoured the shelves of the minimart for jars of baby food and convenient little cookies and baby biscuits for the day. As if my sisters, Patti and Ann, could not have figured out how to keep a one-year-old alive for a couple hours. They had five kids between them, not to mention the fact that they had helped raise me. It was the wedding-day jitters that seemed to be uncorking my usually contained mother lode of control freakiness.

I had made Stella's outfit by hand. Please note that I wrote "made" and not "sewn." Why bother with a needle and thread when you possess an arsenal of hot glue guns? No, I did not lose my mind and bedazzle a onesie for the occasion. Okay . . . define "bedazzle." I attached some rosettes to a onesie, and fashioned a detachable white tulle skirt with free-floating silk flower petals that I had hand-painted to match Sissy's skirt.

I worried about Stella missing me while I got ready. I worried about me missing Stella. I worried about her outfit coming unglued. I worried about her aunts coming unglued. I worried that the un-potty-trained Stella would accidentally put some of her own design touches on her outfit.

In the middle of all this worrying, I turned a corner to see John in the potato chip aisle. Apparently his main concern was figuring out what snacks our brothers, his best man Joe Landon, and he would be taking with them on the forty-five-minute drive to the wedding. He smiled and gave me the thumbs-up, showing me his shopping cart full of limo provisions, which included a collection of every flavor of fat-free Pringles. NEW—WITH OLESTRA. I dove for the cart and started restacking the Pringles cans onto the shelf. He was pretty miffed until I pointed out the warning label: OLESTRA MAY CAUSE ANAL LEAKAGE. My wedding flashed before my eyes. I had averted the major catastrophe of five grown men batching their tuxedo slacks during the ceremony. Pick your battles. Stella would be fine.

Let the games begin. I knew not to tempt fate. Any attempt to straighten my hair for the wedding would be in vain. The unholy alliance of my paternal genetics and the Ohio Valley humidity would make resistance futile. My only hope was the one-two punch of Roger, professional makeup artist and hairdresser, combined with Sissy, whose no-nonsense style had never allowed her own hair to grow beyond three inches since I had known her. They refused to be bested. Armed with a curling iron each and fortified with fish sandwiches and vanilla Cokes from Frisch's Big Boy, they achieved the impossible by wrestling my unruly locks into place. Okay, so there were concessions made. Yes, there were curls. But they were on my terms.

Our out-of-town guests packed onto a party bus outside the hotel in downtown Cincinnati. They ended up having to brave the hometown crowds that had gathered, as they do one weekend every September, for Oktoberfest. It was not my intention to expose my guests to the hazards of oompah-pah bands and beer stein–wielding Cincinnatians attempting impromptu chicken dances in the streets. Not until that morning when I had spied an early-rising reveler decked out in lederhosen and a Cincinnati Reds baseball cap did it dawn on me that our festivities would be occurring simultaneously.

The wedding was officiated by the mayor of Wilmington at the time, Nick Eveland. All went without a hitch. Except for the fact that it dawned on John about halfway through the ceremony that we were actors standing onstage. I saw a look come over him. John had gotten the urge to give the crowd their money's worth. As the four-piece combo played "Come Rain or Come Shine," he swept me up in his arms and began to dance with me. He gave Joe the nod. Joe grabbed Sissy and started to twirl her around the stage. The song went longer than anyone expected. John ended up tapping Joe on the shoulder and cutting in, so I ended up finishing the dance with the best man. John later told me that he had to ham it up because it was agonizing for him to stand still on a stage for that long.

When we exchanged rings, it was immediately apparent to me that John had literally *exchanged* my ring. John had switched the simple silver band we had picked out. He was putting a ring on my finger that was covered in little tiny diamonds. I was in shock. I said, "It's beautiful," out loud, without even knowing it. Then I forgot my lines. Fortunately, I just had to repeat after the mayor. John was not a jewelry-wearing kind of guy. He assured me that after the wedding it was very unlikely that he would wear the ring, and asked me not to buy him an expensive one. So I didn't. I mean, I really did not. His ring cost me $137. But the inscription was priceless.

Four years before, New Year's 1995, John and I had made a trip to New Orleans. Again with the timing—we ended up in the city during the Sugar Bowl. We roamed the streets together, occasionally having to cling to each other so as not to be pulled in separate directions by waves of college football fans. Despite the massive crowds, we were overjoyed to be in New Orleans, a city we both loved but had never gotten to explore together.

On our final morning there, for whatever reason, our wake-up call did not come through. We both sat up from a deep sleep at the same time, looked at the clock and started swearing and getting dressed, knowing that more than likely we were going to miss our plane. Luckily, we had packed the night before. John was a good influence on me that way (incidentally, the effect has worn off). We bolted down to the lobby in record time. There was not a doorman in sight. Nothing but a sea of humanity. Every tourist seemed to be leaving the city at the same time. The football game was over and everyone was making a mad dash to the airport.

John and I split off and were both trying to hail cabs at the same time. In our attempt to double our chances of success, we had lost each other in the throng. When I finally got a cab to stop, I fruitlessly scanned the crowd for John before getting in. I quickly decided this was probably the last helicopter out of Saigon and I should snag it and then drive around in hopes of finding him. I flung open the door and jumped in the backseat, smashing into some jerk who had simultaneously jumped in the other door. The cab driver was saying, "You all goin' to the airport?" as it dawned on me that the cab-stealing jerk was John.

Before I could open my mouth, John was smiling at me like the cat that swallowed the improv canary. This could be dangerous. I knew that look. John said to me, "I'm going to the airport, are you, ma'am?"

I hesitated for a moment, but when I saw how much John was enjoying this bit, I said, "Yes, I'm going to the airport. Do you want to share the cab?" It was on.

John introduced himself, saying his name was Bill Parrot and that he had been traveling on business from Encino. Astonished, I replied that I, too, lived in Encino and had also been in New Orleans on business. Then we both said, "What are the chances?" at the same time. We laughed. Then we overlaughed. Then our mutual laughter trailed off into awkward silence, as we both turned away and looked out our windows.

The driver let out a knowing sigh. This was not the first time he'd had to help move things along in his backseat. He pushed back the brim of his cap and swiveled his head to look at us over his shoulder. Until then, our view of him had consisted solely of the back of his wide pink neck, which time and sun had apparently transformed into Spam. In the thickest New Orleans drawl I had ever heard outside of *A Streetcar Named Desire*, he introduced himself. "My name's Johnny." He flashed a smile and winked a crinkly blue eye at me. Then he proceeded to ask me if I was married. I said "No." Then he asked Bill Parrot if he, too, was single. Bill Parrot confirmed that he was.

He seemed happy with this development and piped up with, "Well, then you two be freezin' da bird." John and I looked at each other. Obviously, this was a slightly dirty Southern colloquialism that Tennessee Williams had never let the world in on. Johnny went on to explain to us (as best as we could tell) that we two should exchange numbers. Because we were both currently unattached, there was nothing holding us back. We're freezin' da bird. It finally dawned on us that we had misunderstood him. Apparently, he was reminding us that we were both "free as a bird."

Bill Parrot said, "You're right," and pulled me in for a kiss. Major lip lock ensued. Johnny the cab driver struggled to keep his eyes on the road. Then, after a few peeks at us in the rearview mirror, he couldn't help but smile at his job well done. He let out under his breath, "Daaaaat's right."

After the wedding ceremony we emerged with Stella to a hail of popcorn being thrown instead of rice. (Okay, Sissy didn't do it all. The popcorn was my idea.) Our limo peeled out from in front of the Murphy Theater and we weren't five minutes out of town when Stella started crying to get out of her car seat. Our car pulled over and John unbuckled our baby and sat her on my lap. In that quiet moment alone with my baby and . . . husband . . . Wow, it all caught up with me. We had just gotten married. This was our honeymoon. John sat cross-legged on the floor in front of us beaming, while I nursed Stella to sleep. I whispered to John to check out the inscription inside his ring. *Daaaaat's Right.*

He wore it.

chapter 17

Big Abenture

A few weeks after our wedding, John was asked to read for Neil Simon's new play *The Dinner Party*. John, along with most everybody in America, was a huge Neil Simon fan. When he got the script in his hands he got right to work. He read it through several times and wrote copious notes in the margins. He asked me to teach him his lines. As long as I had known him, he was always wildly appreciative of my memorizing techniques. He, above everyone else, appreciated the mnemonic devices I laboriously crafted to cue the next bit of dialogue for myself. For me, this technique was a necessity due to the "interesting" way that my brain works. For John, it was an entertaining and helpful shortcut.

Lines learned: John was still not feeling great about the upcoming audition. An ardent Simon admirer, John thought his zeal would get in the way of delivering the comedy goods. He asked for and received brilliant advice from his manager, the legendary Bernie Brillstein. Bernie suggested that John read Neil's memoir, *Rewrites,* if he really wanted to know how he liked his lines served up and what he expected from his actors. John bought the book and read it straight through, annotating and bookmarking as he went.

John had always said that the quality that he found most fascinating about Neil Simon's writing is that you never knew what was coming around the corner. "It could be a parade or it could be a big Mack truck." The fundamental lesson that John took away from the book was simple but profound. Basically, *if you're going to say something funny, you don't have to say it in a funny way.* John committed himself to delivering the lines completely realistically. He would *say* Neil's funny words as opposed to trying to sell it, put a little English on it or joke it up. He trusted the material completely.

John's dear friend and United Cerebral Palsy telethon cohost Henry Winkler had already been cast in the six-person play. John and Henry had been friends ever since *Happy Days* and *Three's Company* were neck-and-neck in the ratings. They had worked together in just about every show-biz venue, even starring in an ABC TV movie together. The 1993 domestic drama featured John's character protecting his wife from her menacing first husband, played by Henry. The climax of the film involved the two real-life friends in a fight to the death in the kitchen. I made sure I was there for the day-long choreographing and filming of the scene—nobody wants to miss Jack Tripper and the Fonz going berserk on each other with steak knives. During the cast and crew's lunch break, word came down from the network that they wanted to change the name of the movie from *Grounds for Murder*, which seemed fine—sounded like it was about coffee beans—but fine. John asked me to come up with a couple of titles. In light of the scene I had just witnessed, I came up with what I thought were two good titles: *Unhappy Days* or (my favorite) *Three's Cutlery*. Sadly, they went with my third suggestion of *The Only Way Out*, not to be—make that *forever to be*—confused with the Kevin Costner spy movie of basically the same name.

As far as John knew, his buddy Henry was unaware that he would be reading for the role in the play. Feeling very vulnerable at the prospect of auditioning for America's most venerable comedic playwright, John didn't want Henry to know until it was over. The morning of the big audition I wished him luck, kissed him good-bye, and then—if I remember this correctly—I held my breath for three hours.

When John returned home, he opened the kitchen door and looked just at me. He stood there. I said, "Well? How did it go?" He said, "I don't know, I think maybe I got the part." I said, "Really? What did they say to you?" And he said, "that I got the part." I said, "John, you got the part." His face lit up. Then there was dancing, oh the dancing. Knocked-kneed, pigeon-toed, super-funky, scrunch-faced, lip-biting, fanny-wagging dancing. He later told me that he had been so relieved that he had not humiliated himself in front of Neil Simon, he hadn't really thought beyond their meeting. He hadn't really been able to fully process the fact that he got the role until he was back in our kitchen.

John, Henry, and the Los Angeles cast worked diligently under the direction of John Rando. *The Dinner Party* opened at the Mark Taper Forum on November 28, 1999. It was one of those magical nights that only theater can provide. Actual human beings, live and in person, attempting to demonstrate and re-create what connects us all, for a hundred minutes with no intermission. They killed. (That's a good thing. Like gladiators, actors either kill or get killed.)

I was revved up to duck backstage after the show and congratulate him. I ran up to him and threw my arms around him, and before I could say anything, he kissed me and said, "Amy, that was hilarious." I had no idea what he was talking about, forgetting I had sent an opening night present backstage before the show. It was a big bouquet of roses and a book. The book was a full-color catalog of the 1970s feminist artist Judy Chicago's seminal work, also named *The Dinner Party*. Chicago's Dinner Party is an art installation comprised of a huge ceremonial banquet table set with porcelain plates that are all surrealistic, three-dimensional representations of the genitalia of prominent historical women. On the first page, I had lovingly inscribed:

John~
> *Kisses on your opening . . .*
>> *Love, Amy*

My husband was famous for occasionally taking things "a joke too far." He always told people that I had written:

John~

Kisses on YOUR opening, for a change . . .

Love, Amy

The show in Los Angeles turned out to be a big hit. After their scheduled run downtown at the Taper, the cast was invited to perform the play that summer at the Kennedy Center in Washington, D.C. While there, they learned that they would be going to Broadway in the fall. John was alternately glowing and glowering for the rest of the summer. Besides the obvious thrill of performing on Broadway, there were major logistic concerns. The upside of us moving to New York was that two of John's kids were already living there. Jason was entering his junior year at New York University studying drama. And Carly was in Poughkeepsie, a mere ninety minutes away by train, starting her freshman year at Vassar. The downside, and a huge one, was moving all the way across the country from Tyler, who was a sophomore in high school. I knew this would be a heartbreaking separation for both of them.

As September 2000 grew near, we started to grasp the reality of our pending "big abenture," a term coined early on by Baby Stella's attempt to imitate her Dad's excited proclamation any time they set out together. Whether it was their trip to Universal Studios or an early-morning coffee run or a walk to the mailbox, every journey was preceded by John asking Stella if she was ready for the *big adventure*. Over time, he gave in and began pronouncing it her way. Once John had made peace with the fact that the three of us were really moving to New York, he let himself get very excited.

The difference between being the star of a TV sitcom and starring in a Broadway play was the difference between being the beloved class clown and being the president of the student council. John had managed to achieve both titles while still in high school and he knew the difference. Aside from the absolute kick-ass joy of it, the credibility that a run on Broadway brings is something to which most actors aspire. In fact, most industry newspapers, including *Variety,* still refer to live theater as "legit"—no offense intended to the rest of us screen bastards, I'm sure.

No one was more grateful to have a shot on Broadway than John was. Five years before, as Markie and Michael and I were trying not to completely dork out in Jerry Lewis's dressing room, Jerry took John aside. He put his arm around John's shoulder and pointed out the picture he had hung on the wall of his father, Danny Lewis. He told John that in spite of all of his accolades and success in film and television and his stage work with Dean Martin, his father always let him know that you haven't really made it until you've been on Broadway. He told John that on opening night of *Damn Yankees,* as he was standing on the elevator contraption waiting for his rise up through the floor of the stage to make his entrance, he felt his father's presence and he said to himself, "Okay, Dad, this is it." John said that it touched him deeply that Jerry had shared that with him. And I think John himself felt much the same way. He was chomping at the bit to walk the boards of The Great White Way.

But first we had to move. John was a California boy through and through, and as much as he loved visiting New York in every season, I knew the move and the weather would be an enormous hassle. I had never felt so "L.A." as when I was preparing to leave. I hadn't even packed one box of clothes and I was already wracked with separation anxiety. The layering alone was guaranteed to drive me crazy. Stella had never let me zip her into the flimsiest of jackets without a tense power struggle that would inevitably end in tears—yes, mine.

Hardy East Coasters love to joke about West Coasters having thin blood. Well, I had unashamedly grown accustomed to the blush-colored, watery fluid running through my veins. I was used to the L.A. version of weather preparedness. Surely, somewhere in the "way back" of my car, the requisite threadbare cardigan lay abandoned. John had never lived through the seasons in Manhattan; I had. New York, New York (the town so nice I lived there twice)—I knew whatever romantic Currier and Ives image John had of the city as a sparkling, snow-covered wonderland would disappear faster than you can say "gray slush."

Stella and I joined John in New York at the end of September. His first morning off work we all set out from our apartment on West Fifty-seventh Street for a walk through Central Park. We rode on the carousel, fed the squirrels, climbed the rocks, and wandered around, lost for the most part. Then a weird thing happened. Stella was the first one of us to sense the vibe. She grabbed ahold of John's hand and began to pull him toward a kind of hum we were now all hearing in the distance. Stella acted as our divining rod as she led us around a grove of trees and toward a gathering of people. People in business suits, hippie-dippie people, mamas with strollers. Turns out, we had unknowingly looped around and now found ourselves in Strawberry Fields at the *Imagine* mosaic created to honor John Lennon. It was October 9, Lennon's birthday. Folks were strumming guitars and singing "Give Peace a Chance." Little children were playing with the flowers that had been strewn around the memorial. And "incense" was curling up into the early autumn air while park rangers pretended not to notice.

The look on John's face when we realized what day it was and where we had found ourselves spoke volumes. He felt that this meant that our relocation to New York City was meant to be. As M. Night Shyamalan pointed out in his movie *Signs,* in some way the world comes down to two different kinds of people: those who believe in signs and those who don't. John was for the most part a believer and I was . . . well, not so much. Signs don't just pop up; signs are deliberately put in your path. Believing in signs would mean that somebody else has got control of all of this. That was a comfort to him. He felt that the three of us landing in Strawberry Fields meant everything was gonna be okay. He took it as an indication that because his hero, John Lennon, had loved New York City, this may just be a little nod from him. Our move to New York had been officially Beatles approved.

As fall progressed, the Strawberry Fields feeling began to fade. Now was the winter of my disconnect. We had moved to New York in the middle of my attempt at the unfashionably late weaning of my two-year-old. She was recently potty trained, for which I was very grateful, but I knew in my heart that our giant pickup and schlep to the East Coast would most likely undo both of those milestones. I didn't know when the pushback would happen, but I was fully expecting and prepared for a little passive regression on Stella's part. What I hadn't bargained for was how much living in New York would blow John's mind. It's not exactly like he started nursing and pooping his pants—not exactly. Instead, he began to exhibit a very faraway look in his eyes any time he wasn't actively engaged. In fact, for the duration of the ten months we lived in New York, John's default setting was melancholy.

Although John spoke to Tyler on the phone almost every day and flew him to New York whenever his high school schedule allowed, he missed his boy something awful. One clock in our apartment was always set to L.A. time, Tyler time. Finding phone call time when John's job and Tyler's school schedules jibed was a priority. The few instances that I saw John get really angry while we were in New York had to do with the frustration of having to miss one of those precious windows.

During winter break from school, Tyler came to stay with us for a while. Stella was more than a little excited to have her big bro all to herself. Every morning, as Tyler slept, facedown and out for the count on our surprisingly cozy inflatable mattress, she would bolt from her bed in her flannel pjs, run into the living room, and dive onto him. I intervened once in an attempt to delay his usual wake-up call and give him some much needed extra Zs. That morning, I scooped Stella up, mid-dash, and plopped her in the tub for an early bath.

Just as I was rinsing her off, John squeezed into the tiny bathroom to ask what was going on. Considering the theater schedule to which we had all become accustomed, to us 6:00 a.m. was the middle of the night. I handed him the wet, squirming Stella and a towel and said I was going back to sleep. I had just slid under the covers when I heard a lot of noises emanating from the living room: Tyler's horrified scream, squealing, laughter, more laughter . . . and more laughter. Apparently, Stella, fresh from her bath, and naked as the day she was born, had broken free from John and made a beeline for her sleeping brother.

John threw a towel on her and sat her down for a serious conversation. He was great at getting his point across to his kids without totally humiliating them in the process. He never talked down to Stella and she always came away from one of their serious talks enlightened. On every big abenture you learn a lesson or two on the way. I know he made quite an impression on her that morning. For the rest of our time in New York, she would always pipe up with the same answer when we would ask her, "What are the two most important things in life?" In all seriousness and without hesitation, she would answer: "Boundaries and pants."

chapter 18

Broadway, Baby

John was, inarguably, the biggest baseball fan in the world. His beloved Dodgers were out of the playoffs for the season, so finding himself in New York during the 2000 World Series between the Mets and the Yankees, he decided to jump in with both . . . hats. During the Subway Series, whenever John was in public he would carry both a Yankees and a Mets cap with him at all times. Sometimes he'd wear them on top of each other. If a Yankee fan seemed pissed off to see John Ritter in a Mets cap, or vice versa, he'd swap it out right then and there. His buddy Joe would have chalked this up to his perpetual campaign for student council: "Hi (*firm handshake*), I'm John Ritter and I'm running for class president. I sure would appreciate your vote (*winning smile*)." He readily admitted at the time that his dual loyalties came off like a politically correct Cirque du Soleil backbend in an attempt to accommodate everyone. But the truth is, he just didn't want to miss any of the fun.

Especially amused were all the beat cops he got to know on his walk to work every day. A couple times he even got called over to mediate exaggerated baseball disagreements between partners. He would represent both sides, switching team loyalties as deftly as he did their hats. "Hi, I'm John Ritter and I'm running for president of Broadway . . ."

When Thanksgiving rolled around, we realized that we had inadvertently rented an apartment that was situated perfectly for viewing the parade. Good thing, too; that year, the Macy's Thanksgiving Day Parade boasted a Clifford balloon, Stella's favorite. We would have been very happy—and warm and dry—watching the parade go by from our ninth-floor perch. However, Al Roker had other ideas. He asked if John would be interviewed at the start of the parade route on Seventy-seventh Street and Central Park West. Talk about an offer you couldn't refuse . . . it was thrilling for us to experience the glitzy grandeur up close and personal.

Then, after John's (and Stella's) live TV interview with Al, we slammed the stroller into high gear and began racing the twenty blocks back to our place in hopes of making it to Fifty-seventh Street before Clifford did. With more than a dozen barricades in front of us, the prospects looked dim. The parade route was understandably locked down and heavily guarded by New York's finest. I'm sure some of the police officers would've escorted us past a barricade or two because we seemed like nice people. And I'm sure even more of them would have let us through because they had recognized John. But *all* of them?

Apparently—and this is no surprise to anyone who knew him—John had made friends with every cop he encountered in the previous three months on his daily walk to work. And the word spread: *This guy is for real.* He had engendered an enormous amount of goodwill just by being himself. And when he did that, as usual, barriers of every kind seemed to disappear. Even with all the handshaking and picture taking, we made it home, raced into the lobby, up the elevator, through the apartment door, and to our window just in time to see our boy, Clifford, being walked by a dozen handlers around Columbus Circle and down Broadway.

Speaking of Broadway, Neil Simon's *The Dinner Party* was a success from opening night. Theater veterans Penny Fuller, Len Cariou, Veanne Cox, and Jan Maxwell made TV veterans John and Henry feel right at home. They were warmly welcomed by the New York audiences, as well. John said that he realized it sounded corny, but that it truly meant the world to him to be embraced by the Broadway community so fully.

Once a year, the New York theater community raises funds for Broadway Cares, the nation's leading industry-based HIV/AIDS fund-raising organization. Every play makes a pitch from the stage at the end of their show for donations. Every show does it a little differently, and usually the big shows, like *Annie Get Your Gun,* have the actors shake the can for funds after the show. Well, John and Henry, being the experienced telethon duo that they were, decided to take it up a notch . . . or ten. Taking advantage of the relatively short running time of the show, the six-member cast would come back out on stage after the final curtain and put on a little after-show show.

They would deliver their scripted spiel for the charity (tourists who were theater-hopping for a couple of weeks probably knew it by rote) and then they would take questions from the audience. After the Q&A session, they would then turn over the stage to John and Henry to host an improvised auction for their (literally) captive audience. The rapt (trapped) spectators would be cajoled and encouraged to bid on tours of the dressing rooms, pictures with the cast, hugs, pieces of the set (much to the chagrin of the set crew), and pieces of the casts' wardrobe (wisely limited to replaceable handkerchiefs after some good-natured chastising brought John and Henry to their senses). The upshot of this fire sale/kissing booth was the raising of a record-breaking amount of money. The combined effect of *The Dinner Party* cast caring so deeply, and their appreciative audiences digging so deeply, resulted in the largest amount of money ever raised for Broadway Cares by a nonmusical. John was as proud of that as he was of his work in the play.

While we were living in New York City, we were all invited to the premiere of the Disney movie *102 Dalmatians*. In anticipation of the movie's release and Halloween, the Disney Store (where Stella and I were regular browsers) had made sure that the purchasing public knew that Dalmatian was the new black. I bought Stella the little zip-up black-and-white fake-fleece size-two costume, which completely covered every part of her, aside from her face, hands, and feet. It even had a little red felt collar with a dog tag to complete the look. Little did I know that I would be handwashing that sucker every couple of days for the next four months. Stella wore it to the premiere and then never took it off. As I had anticipated, she flat-out refused to wear every piece of cold-weather clothing I had tried to charm, goad, or bribe her into. The costume, with mittens (paws) safety pinned to the sleeves, was the only winter wear she didn't reject. Nonplussed New Yorkers hardly gave it a second glance.

For the most part, our daily routine started at noon, when we would wake up and roll back the blackout blinds. Most days, John would start out for work around 4:00 p.m. and Stella and I would take the B train uptown. Especially convenient on days when the whole of aboveground Manhattan was snowed in, Stella and I would ride a couple stops until the subway doors would open onto the lower level of the Museum of Natural History. That was our playground. Nurture or nature, this kid was turning out to be a chip off the old nerd-block. Neither one of us ever tired of the place.

At the beginning, she would ask me questions about the exhibits in her teeny little voice and I would just read her the answers from the labels. Little by little, both of us began inadvertently memorizing the information. For me, this experience served as a wildly enjoyable, finally absorbable, "post-college" science course. For Stella, it was Oz, Wonderland, and the Magic School Bus all rolled into one. After a while, the docents knew her by name and allowed us to tag along on their tours;

the curators and exhibit designers got used to us, as well. Only once was there a small incident involving a complaint about us by a new volunteer tour guide. Apparently, she didn't take kindly to having her pronunciation of "Neanderthal" questioned by a Dalmatian. But who does, really?

When the museum would close at seven o'clock, we would make our way down to the Barnes & Noble at Sixty-sixth and Broadway. We always enjoyed ourselves and sometimes the staff would even have books waiting for Stella that they knew she'd get a kick out of. At some point, usually around nine-ish, I would be faced with the inevitable headshake/tongue cluck/question from a customer about having a baby (puppy) out so late. I was usually able to reassure them with a fake exasperated eye-roll, a goofy mom smile toward Stella, and an exhausted, "Oh, I know . . . we're on L.A. time." True enough, but we had moved to New York months before.

The fact that I had synched up Stella's and John's schedules so we could optimize the time they got to spend together before and after his theater workday was not a conversation I was willing to have with strangers. Truth was, I didn't really care about their opinions. And had I been pushed, I would've said so. Most folks would quickly do the time zone math in their heads and walk away, curiosity satisfied. There was a subset of the bookstore-going public, however, that really put the "mean" in well-meaning. I would sense them screwing up their courage and adjusting their pearls, as they tore themselves away from the cookbook section to make a beeline for the horrible mother and her poor little child.

I began to realize that around 11:00 p.m. my West Coast excuse did start to lose credibility. After a while, I began to invoke even more westerly time zones. I really hadn't been aware of how much of this deflecting Stella had absorbed. But sure enough, by that December, she had begun to pre-empt any and all judgment of her schedule or lack thereof. Stella would meet any woman in a matching sweater set who dared to venture into the children's book section with a fake smile and a reassuring, "Hawaii time."

In the spring, John joined the Broadway Softball League. Most of the teams were from huge musicals. *Annie Get Your Gun* and *Phantom of the Opera* had very deep rosters from which to pull. *The Dinner Party,* on the other hand, was a six-person ensemble piece. They joined forces (farces?) with a brilliant Irish play called *Stones in His Pockets* that was running concurrently on Forty-fifth Street and a softball team was born. *"Party in His Pockets"* did pretty well that season; I just wish they had teamed up with the two Australian actors who had burst onto the Broadway-ish scene with their (two-hander) master . . . piece called *Puppetry of the Penis.* I have no idea if those guys knew how to play baseball. I just liked the idea of the sports section headline: PENIS PARTY UPSETS JANE EYRE IN LATE NIGHT DOUBLEHEADER!

At the beginning of the summer, John and Henry ended their run in the play and their roles were filled by Larry Miller and Jon Lovitz, respectively. Stella and I had flown home a couple weeks earlier to prepare for Dad's return. John called from JFK before he boarded the flight to Los Angeles and told me that he had shaved off his beard that morning. Never thinking she would be anything other than intrigued, I passed that information on to Stella. No less shaken than if I had said, "Jack Tripper's coming home instead of Dad," Stella was freaked. Not a fan of change at that time, this was the worst thing she'd ever heard. She convinced herself that it would possibly grow back during the flight home. I tried everything I could think of to make it okay for her, to no avail.

Hours later, John, who had picked up Tyler on his way over, called from the car. I told them both what was going on. Tyler said he would come upstairs to her room to talk to her when they arrived. When Stella heard them come through the front door, she dove behind her floor-length bedroom curtains to hide. Tyler came in and coaxed her out with a hug and big-brotherly reassurance. Tyler said, "Daddy just wants you to come downstairs. You don't have to look at him, just listen to his voice."

So Tyler carried Stella down the stairs; she clung to him with her head buried in his chest. I watched from the second-floor landing, as John stood next to them and talked to Stella, telling her to reach out her hand. As he was talking, he took her hand and held it to his face so she could hear his voice and feel his cheeks at the same time. She turned her head to the side and rested it on Tyler's shoulder. I saw from my perch that she was peeking through one eye at John. When she couldn't stand it anymore, she jumped into her dad's arms, put both hands on his smooth cheeks, and squeezed his face into a fishy kiss. She laid one on him and then initiated a group hug. She didn't let go of John for about two whole days. She was thrilled that we were all back home together.

chapter 19

Who Knew?

John very rarely lectured me about anything. Good thing, too. Growing up with such a vast age difference between my siblings and me had rendered me extremely wary of anyone trying to pull rank. My brothers and sisters never tried, but I like to think I would've been ready for them if they had. I lost both of my parents by the time I was twenty-one and I was nobody's baby. When John and I first met, he called me "Kid." Once. I hit him with both barrels. It didn't happen again. I was fourteen years younger than he was and it irked me that he saw me as a kid. I later realized that he and his best friends referred to one another that way and it was a term of endearment coming from him.

Over time, I eased up on my knee-jerk reaction to anything that smacked of condescension. Luckily, I got out of my own way on that one fairly early on in our relationship. I learned to be able to accept his advice in the spirit in which he was giving it. And it went both ways. I gave as good (heartedly) as I got.

The best advice he ever gave me is still some of the hardest to take. Right after we moved back to Los Angeles from our big abenture in New York, he pointed out the boxes and boxes of photographs and videotapes I had taken during our stay. He said, "Be careful with that." The "that" he was referring to was my tendency to see everything through a camera lens. Stella was about to start nursery school, and he cautioned me that I could miss a lot if I was constantly concerned with framing the action. He said, "You are going to miss the whole experience of being there. It's so much better to be fully *there* than to capture a moment or two." His advice sounded hippie-ish and actor-y . . . and true.

In the early morning of September 11, 2001, my sister Ann called from Cincinnati to tell us to turn on our television. The destruction and horror of what was happening slowly sunk in. John was on the phone making sure the big kids were safe. Tyler was home with his mom; Jason, though he had been going to school in New York, was spending a semester in London; Carly was in New York, but upstate in Poughkeepsie at Vassar. We watched the morning unfold together and cried and generally freaked out . . . but softly. We knew at some point Stella would wake up. September 11, 2001, also happened to be her third birthday. She had gone to sleep grudgingly the night before, full of anticipation and questions for us, about what turning three really meant and how her world would be different. We watched from the doorway as she slept, curled up, angel faced, and innocently unaware that the world had changed forever. Quietly, John and I lay down on either side of her and had a conversation with each other that brought me peace in that moment and that just may last me a lifetime, like a well that I can go to again and again.

I asked him how we could do this. How could we say "Happy Birthday" when we knew that this day would always be the anniversary of the day this evil thing happened? Without hesitating, he said, "Stella is proof that love still exists in the world, that somehow, we go on."

He really believed that sharing her birthday with this day of mourning may serve to make her wiser and stronger because it would force her to recognize the full scope of our human experience. I wanted to argue the point a little, but I couldn't. I wanted so much to believe it. And I would have to, if I was ever going to sell his philosophy to Stella.

When Stella woke up, we put on the Disney Channel, and sat her in front of it. We went in the other room and gathered ourselves. CNN was on downstairs and Disney's *House of Mouse* was on upstairs. We tried, to the best of our abilities, to protect her from the tragedy.

Later on in the day, our friend Jay Ginsberg came by with a birthday present for Stella. The four of us went to Jerry's Deli and sat stunned, like everyone else in the place, watching the news. I sat Stella in one of the few seats in that restaurant that does not have a direct view of a television.

As we tried to eat, John and I reminisced about another restaurant, Windows on the World. That past May, John had been nominated for a daytime Emmy for best performer in an animated series for his work on *Clifford: The Big Red Dog*. All of the Emmy nominees for 2001 were invited to a ceremony and reception honoring them at the mayor's office. The three of us mixed and mingled with the soap opera crowd. But instead of staying for the food, John, Stella, and I set out to visit the World Trade Center, which none of us had ever seen up close. John hoisted Stella on his shoulders and we set off on our journey toward the Twin Towers.

After an ear-popping elevator ride to the top of the North Tower, we found ourselves wandering into Windows on the World. It was early and the restaurant wasn't open yet, but that didn't stop the staff from welcoming us in for a tour. Chef Michael Lomonaco came out and shook John's hand. It was just like all of the warm receptions John had received from restaurateurs all over the world. John was as happy to meet and greet these folks as they were to meet him.

Across the restaurant, Stella stood spellbound with her palms and nose pressed up against the 106th-story window. Patiently standing next to her was a woman with a squeegee and a bottle of Windex. Apparently, Stella had just smudged one of the most famous windows in Manhattan. John and I rushed up behind her in an effort to peel her off the glass. She said to us, without turning around, "But I feel like I'm in the clouds!" The woman with the squeegee sweetly waved us away saying, "I know, I feel like that every day up here."

Sitting there at the deli with Jay and Stella, John and I had no way of knowing if we had lost anyone we knew. After making New York our home for the last year, we had returned home to Los Angeles with a phonebook full of numbers. None of them seemed to be working. The full scope of the tragedy was now rapidly being revealed. The bartender reached up and adjusted the volume so everyone in the place could hear. We learned that all seventy-three people who were at work on September 11 at Windows on the World perished in the attack.

That night, with the volume turned all the way down, John and I watched the images of the towers falling over and over again. We sat side by side on our couch. As Stella slept stretched out across both of our laps, a clock blinked on somewhere, unnoticed, and began its countdown. We had exactly two years left together from that night. Who knew?

Stella was three, and she was ready to try out a little independent time. I, on the other hand, was freaking out that my little baby would be without me three hours a day, five days a week. We had decided to send Stella to a co-op nursery school. This meant that we would be expected to volunteer in the classroom at least twice a month. It also meant that we were expected to be involved in everything from the upkeep of the school, to the fund-raising, to the wiping of noses and bottoms of other peoples' toddlers. I was not down with O.P.T. (yeah, you know me). This is where I learned to ignore my supersensitive sense of smell. If I can pretend not to be aware of your kid's poopy Pull-Up, I can avoid having to change it.

A week before school started, John attended an orientation event where parents of incoming students mingled with the alumni. When he came home from the meeting, he looked at me and said, "Two words: Peter. Higgins." Peter's son Mickey had recently graduated from the program, so he knew all the ins and outs of daily life at the school. He had the goods on everybody and they knew it. John was right; Peter was clearly the go-to guy.

Just starting her first year at the school was his daughter, Lucy. She and Stella became fast friends—good thing, because at their very first play date Peter and I bonded immediately. My recollection is that his big, brash Irish sense of humor resonated with me, being the half Murphy that I proudly am. Erin go bragh-less. His recollection is that he admired how deftly and unapologetically I employed the C-word in reference to a particularly difficult actress. It was a proud day for the Irish—of whom Freud was purported to have said, "This is *one race* of people for whom psychoanalysis is of no use whatsoever." Despite that fact, or more likely because of it, Peter and I became inseparable friends.

In the summer of 2002, John agreed to do a photo shoot in our backyard for Scholastic, the publisher for the *Clifford* book series and producer of the PBS show. Clifford had been introduced into our lives—well, reintroduced in my case—when Stella was a tiny baby. John swore that he had, honest to God, never heard of the book when he was asked to voice the part for the PBS cartoon. I always found that incredibly hard to believe. Considering that this guy had read every book I had ever heard of, plus thousands more, I couldn't imagine that he had missed The Big Red Dog.

Ever since I had first read the book in second grade, Clifford had been alive in my imagination. I had even described to my family that going out in public with John was a lot like Emily Elizabeth taking Clifford for a walk. Crowds gathered, people were in awe, they couldn't believe their eyes. Being out on the town with our bigger-than-life partners caused lots of unexpected and interesting problems for both Emily and me. But I know neither one of us would've traded our crazy lives for anything in the world.

John quickly became a fan of the book and its message of respect and friendship. John went on to voice sixty-five episodes of the PBS TV show and an animated feature film. The afternoon of the photo shoot, while Stella sat in front of the refrigerator fruitlessly attempting to wrap an oversize dog bone in tissue paper, an eight-foot-tall red dog ducked into our kitchen. This child, who would soon enough be one of the most humorously cynical beings I would ever know, leapt to her feet and ran to him. The gracious hostess genes that she had inherited from both of her Grandma Dorothys kicked into overdrive. She took his paw and led him outside on an extensive tour of our backyard, where she read him books and he pushed her on the swing. She knew that her dad provided the voice for the cartoon but was polite enough not to ask any questions when the "real" Clifford failed to utter as much as a single "woof" all afternoon.

The photo shoot went off without a hitch. It was as if Stella didn't even know the camera was there. But I'm glad it was. And I'm glad I wasn't wielding it. I got to play and watch and absorb every moment with Stella. Okay, so I snapped a couple of pictures . . . it's hard to teach this old red dog new tricks.

Sometime in the middle of our magical afternoon, the kind folks from Scholastic ended up accepting an invitation, on Clifford's behalf, to Stella's fourth birthday party. We decided to do it up right and go with a Clifford's Animal Park theme. We invited all the kids from her little nursery school and hired an animal wrangler. While I was planning Stella's party, John mentioned to me that the day after Stella's upcoming fourth birthday was to be my fortieth. Thank you for reminding me, John. I was okay with turning forty; as okay as a person can be with hitting a fabled milestone that marks your imminent, gravity-induced careen downhill. Let's just say I was not as miffed as I could have been. I was happy-ish, healthy-ish, and life was good. I had a bright, beautiful, goofy four-year-old . . . and a bright, beautiful, goofy, about-to-turn fifty-three-year-old.

I was expecting the usual birthday night outing at the Souplantation. Those salad slingers sing a nice "Happy Birthday," I tell you. But instead, John said, "Let's throw a party for you, too." I knew enough to agree, pronto. No hemming and hawing on my part. As funny and entertaining as John was, he did not particularly have fun entertaining. I didn't want to give him any time to think about it. I jumped on it. It was a smallish gathering of people in the backyard, with a few tables set up, food, music—the usual deal. But it was our first grown-up party in the five years we had been at our house.

It was a beautiful evening with a couple of surprises. No one there will ever forget our friend Peter belting out a clever rendition of "You're the Top" that he'd had specially customized for my birthday. Much better than the original. Why Cole Porter never thought to rhyme "feta cheese" with "Lebanese" is beyond me. The other thing that I did not see coming was the cake. John had made a big deal out of being in charge of my birthday cake. After dinner, when he finally carried it into the backyard, he looked like the cat that swallowed the canary. When the oversize sheet cake was finally unveiled the inscription read:

This is your chocolate birthday cake
You can share with your friends
Or if you feel a little selfish
You can eat it all by yourself
We will understand.
We all love you and want to say
Have a happy day.
You are great!
With love, admiration and respect
For all that you do in the world,
Happy Birthday, Amy Irving,
Who is now 40 years young.

I had eased up considerably on the picture taking over the previous year, per John's advice. I think the only picture I took at my birthday party was of the cake. Nobody would've believed it, otherwise.

Actually, my rebellious nature had kept me from complying entirely with John's wise counsel. I had snapped hundreds of pictures and taped hours of video of both John and Stella. When I look back now at all the photographs and home movies that I took of them, I realize that I never questioned for a moment who they were for; who the audience would be. For five years—exactly five—every time I picked up a camera, my unspoken intention was to capture Stella in time—for us. Never, in the farthest reaches of my mind, did I envision these images being anything but a mother and father's comfort—John and I, on our couch, watching and rewinding and remembering, in our empty nest after our little bird had flown.

chapter 20

One Simple Rule:
"If That Happens on Show Night,
Just Keep Going!"

Early in 2002, John, Stella, and I took a trip to Florida to visit Disney World and see my sister Ann and her husband, Jim. Disney World with Stella was a blast, and I got to show her where Mommy swam around as a mermaid all those years ago in *Splash, Too.* We stayed in Naples at the Ritz-Carlton, and John had brought some scripts to read for the coming TV season. John always had a pile of prospective TV series scripts, sent by producers and writers, awaiting his perusal. He gave each production his consideration, although he had not been so keen on the idea of jumping back into a half-hour situation comedy. But now that he was the father of a young child again, he wanted a more predictable schedule than guest-starring and film roles afforded him. The world of sitcoms missed him, and John was opening up to the fact that maybe he missed them a little, too.

When we got to the hotel, John tossed a script for an ABC Disney family comedy into a beach bag along with four books and several magazines, and rushed Stella and me out the door with his famous "Here we go!" As I stood onshore with Stella in my arms, she took one look at the waves and started squirming with excitement. Thank God, John was a master at the art of sunscreen application. After all those summers of having to slather his three kids all at once, he had it down to a science—kid number four was not about to get the best of him.

He would gently turn Stella by the top of her head to face him, like he was opening a jar of pickles, and deftly pat dollops of SPF 50 over every inch of her exposed Ritter-pale skin, repeating the word "bink" with every dab. The ritual was inexplicably soothing, like the tranquilizing effect of massaging an alligator's stomach. John would then quickly rub in the sunscreen while laying out the rules of ocean safety, eye to eye, in a very serious tone, like he was the Mick to Stella's Rocky Balboa.

I took Stella out into the water, while John stretched out on the patchwork of hotel towels we had constructed for our headquarters. I saw him pick up the script for a show called *8 Simple Rules for Dating My Teenage Daughter*. His first impression of it was that the title was way too long, and he told me later that he was actually expecting not to like it. John had been offered so many sitcom-dad roles that they all pretty much blended together, and he didn't have much hope that this one would be any better. I watched him give it a cursory read—as in, "bullshit, bullshit, my part"—and he was smiling and laughing to himself. But he didn't spend very much time on it before tossing it back in the beach bag and taking out a book from his ever-present collection of hardcover novels.

John had no qualms about bringing several books with him even on a short jaunt—history, fiction, suspense, biography, politics—not to mention (but I will, just this once) newspapers, comic books, cartoon compilations, graphic novels, *Mad* magazines, and anything else he could get his hands on. Home and abroad, a sizable collection of his partially read books and periodicals could be found in every room. Still, he would often take several trips to the local bookstore once we had reached our destination. Sometimes, he would finish one and give it away to whoever happened to be nearby in an attempt to lighten our luggage for the return trip. Upon returning home, however, he would more often than not go to our neighborhood bookstore to replace the one he had gifted on our trip. John had a remarkable passion for reading that he exuberantly shared with his family and friends. He would always excitedly tell me about whatever book he had just finished reading, making a big deal of stopping short so as not to give away any twists that might spoil the plot for me.

After I had Stella, I often employed a thinly veiled passive-aggressive response that only a frazzled new mother could get away with; I would say, "Honey, why don't you just go ahead and tell me the whole story. You know I'm never going to have chance to read it." John would always smile patiently and put the book up on one of our many bookshelves, while assuring me, "You will." After John died, I found myself collecting his partially read books from every room in our house, as well as from his dressing room and his car.

Never one to dog-ear a page for reference, John saved his place with bookmarks made from everything from shooting schedules to toilet paper. I stacked an armload of these books beside my bed, since sleeping through the night had become a memory at that point. I read the first book, Steve Martin's novel *The Pleasure of My Company* . . . and I felt like John was reading a bedtime story aloud to me. A bedtime story about a man with agonizing, paralyzing obsessive-compulsive disorder and the social worker who loves him, but a bedtime story all the same. When I turned a page about two-thirds of the way through, I found a green plastic sword-shaped toothpick marking the last page he'd read. John must've been interrupted—perhaps he'd been pounced on by a freshly bathed Stella, or remembered that the Dodger game was on, or gotten a phone call from one of his big kids, or decided his nightly bowl of cornflakes was beckoning, or got an offer from his exhausted but amorous wife that he couldn't refuse. And he never read further. But I did. In those first months, setting aside his makeshift bookmark and turning the page was as much of a concession to "moving on" as I could make.

Voracious reader that he was, John was just finishing off the entire pile of scripts he'd lugged down to Florida by the time dinner rolled around. I reminded him that we were supposed to eat at my sister's house in Fort Myers at seven thirty, then I asked him what he thought of the scripts. He answered that there was "nothing there." I think that would have been that, he would've missed the boat, if we hadn't gotten stuck in traffic on the Tamiami Trail and shown up an hour late for dinner with a passed-out Stella in tow. Ann and her husband, Jim, had just finished watching *My Wife and Kids* and began recounting some of Damon Wayans's best lines over dinner.

Ann has one of those laughs that tends to kick into high gear when she gets going, shifting quickly from a laugh to a bray. The more she tries to stop, the more intense it gets. It kind of leaves you wondering whether you should laugh along or open up a can of Heimlich maneuver on her ass. John loved it though. And the more she talked about Damon and how unexpected and outrageous his interactions with his kids were on the show, the more engaged John became. We mused about fathers in general, how they can simultaneously be all-knowing and idiots, and how entertainingly satisfying that is to observe.

Over the course of that conversation, something clicked with John. When we got back to the hotel, he went straight to the *no* pile on the table and pulled out the script for *8 Simple Rules for Dating My Teenage Daughter,* took it over to the couch, and began to reread it with an open mind and a pencil. The pencil was always a positive sign. When John worked on a script, he wrote in the margins and all over the page. He was scribbling and mouthing the words and laughing to himself. I knew he was feeling invested in this character now and was beginning to picture himself in the role. Stella and I kissed him good night and I went to put her to bed. After she fell asleep, I came out and found him sound asleep with his glasses on, pencil in hand, midscribble. I closed the script, knowing that this was the show for John.

The next day, he talked me into taking our three-year-old up with us on a parasail. John could pretty much talk me into anything. And while we were in the air, he told me he was going to tell his agent *yes* on the project.

Viewers who had grown up with John were happy to have him back on prime time. The actor who had entertained them on *Three's Company* for years with his "roommate problems" was back in their living rooms, now playing a married guy with three kids. His character, Paul Hennessy, was tackling the same issues that a lot of the folks were dealing with at home. The show was an instant hit, winning The People's Choice Award for best new comedy in January of 2003.

The awards ceremony was on the same day that we were taping *Hollywood Squares* together for the Valentine's Day show. Henry Winkler was producing it and had added cut-aways before the commercial breaks. The hand-held camera would pan up and around the gigantic tic-tac-toe grid to catch some of the behind-the-scenes chatter. John saw the camera traveling to our box and whispered in my ear to ask him what he liked best about being on the show. I did and he replied, "Not wearing pants." And he wasn't. Henry was very familiar with John's penchant for dropping comedy trou. Not surprisingly, he and his underpants made it on the air. Luckily, Pantless John always came across more Winnie the Pooh than Winnie the Flasher.

The five-episode taping started on time, but we still got behind schedule. The producers had to ask the celebrity couples to forgo a wardrobe change, thereby blowing the game show illusion that we shot over a five-day period. With the help of the *Hollywood Squares* crew and our lead-footed limo driver, we made it to the awards just in time.

This was the big fat year of *My Big Fat Greek Wedding*, produced by Tom Hanks. He and his wife, Rita Wilson, were seated about ten rows in front of us on the aisle. The movie won an award in practically every category, and Tom got up and down off that stage so many times that it got kind of funny. Then the category for Best New Comedy came up and *8 Simple Rules* won. John jumped up, ran down the aisle, and said, "Eat shit, Tom," into his ear on the way to the stage. Tom was still doubled over laughing when John went up and gave one of the most eloquent and gracious acceptance speeches on behalf of any show I'd ever heard.

At the end of August 2003, *8 Simple Rules* returned to production on the Disney Studio lot to begin shooting the second season. John set out for work on his first day back with a load of Stella's toys, including a three-foot-tall teddy bear and a grocery bag full of plastic food in the backseat of his car. When Stella and I showed up to the first show of the 2003 season, we were in for a bit of a surprise. She opened the door to John's dressing room, and he and the teddy bear were already seated at a miniature tea party. John had Stella-ed up half of his dressing room with a little table and chairs borrowed from the set-dressing department. He was perched on a toddler-size chair, teacup in hand, pinky finger extended. He smiled at Stella and said in his fanciest voice, "Oh, dooooo come in." John had also brought a couple pairs of Stella's pajamas. He told her that she could stay later on show nights this season, now that she was turning five.

Over the previous year, John had fallen back in love with television. And the feeling was mutual. Not only did John find himself on the perfect show at the perfect time but he was working with the perfect people. He adored the *8 Simple Rules* characters and the talented cast and crew who brought them to life. And they adored him. Some of his coworkers, by virtue of their youth, were fairly new to the business. They truly appreciated the opportunity to work side by side with one of the most entertaining and grateful actors they would ever meet. They had the opportunity to learn from a true sitcom veteran. His show business advice, whether heartfelt or tongue in cheek, was received gratefully by all of them.

During rehearsals, he often reminded them about his "one simple rule," a rule that was very familiar to us at home. Any time we accidentally poked ourselves in the eye while gesticulating, or burped while telling a dramatic story, or tripped and dropped a plate on the way to the dinner table, John would announce, "Okay, everybody, if that happens on show night, just keep going." The cast of *8 Simple Rules* never knew how prophetic John's motto would be.

chapter 21

When September Ends

"Seven years has gone so fast
Wake me up when September ends"

—GREEN DAY

The morning of September 11, 2003, I woke John up and reminded him of his birthday promise to Stella the night before. She had just started sleeping in her "big girl bed" that summer, and her wish was to wake up the morning she turned five with her dad and her new cat Peekaboo beside her. We had given Stella her birthday present of a rescue tabby kitten three weeks earlier, but it was still too little to sleep with her. And John, in his lifelong role as Tarzan, master of the animals, had been teaching her how to handle her delicate new pet.

John walked down to the kitchen and scooped up the kitten, then climbed the stairs, beaming up at me with a familiar look of delight on his face. He'd been trying to talk me into getting a pet for a long time. I had resisted, knowing that the added responsibilities would inevitably fall to me. But when he enlisted Stella in the campaign, I was a goner—I caved. Luckily, John was not the kind of person to ever say "I told you so!" Not to me, anyway. He was just genuinely happy when something worked out the way he had hoped. John was at his most irresistible when he was happy, charging the atmosphere in our home and in my heart. His bliss was my bliss. It was that way from the moment I first looked into his eyes.

I watched him now as he crawled carefully into Stella's narrow daybed with her kitten in his arms. He managed to settle in without waking her up. I would've gotten in bed with them if I thought I could've fit. Instead, I opted for a seat in the rocking chair across the room, and watched my little family, the one that I had waited for all my life. All three of them seemed to be purring. Together. There are some moments that you know, as they are happening, will live with you forever.

What I could have never imagined was that this would be John's final hour with Stella. He propped himself up on his elbow and winked at me, as if to say, "Watch this." He knew he was about to tenderly deliver our little daughter's wish to wake up with her daddy and her kitty. He whispered, "Good morning, Birthday Girl." Stella barely stirred, still asleep. He gently cleared his throat, grinned at me, then got really close to her ear and said, "Good morning, Birthday Girl!" She started and abruptly flipped over, momentarily squishing Peekaboo, who screeched and sunk her claws into John's arm, instantly prompting him to contort his face into the dorkiest, cross-eyed, silent scream I had ever seen. John and I busted out laughing as he gingerly detached the cat. Stella bolted upright with her eyes closed and a big, silly smile on her face. Blinking awake, she slowly took in the scene and said, "Happy birthday," in her sweet, gravelly morning voice. We all climbed onto the floor to sit on the rug and open a couple of presents. The rest were to be opened that night when John and I got back from the parents-only back-to-school night. I remember thinking, *what shitty timing* . . .

John got ready to go to his scheduled workout and then drive over the hill to the Disney Studio. It was Thursday and *8 Simple Rules* would be shooting in front of an audience the following night. Peter Bogdanovich and Henry Winkler were guest-starring in that week's episode. John had been cutting up and playing with his two good old friends since Monday. He told me that he was going to try not to goof around so much, so they could plow through rehearsal as quickly as possible. John made sure that everyone on set knew that it was Stella's birthday and that after work he had to drive across town to back-to-school night and then back home before she fell asleep.

In the late afternoon, John was taken across the street to the hospital and admitted into the emergency room with nausea and chest pains. It was assumed that he was having a heart attack. Later that night, while he was being treated for a heart attack he wasn't having, John died of an acute aortic dissection.

I would love to be able to say that the ensuing hours, days, and weeks were a blur. They were not and still are not. My memories are sharp and time has not served to dull their dangerous edges. The images have not arranged themselves into a presentable impressionistic pastiche. Every family who

has been where we found ourselves that September under-
stands. Those of us who have lost—are lost for words.

After the devastation that we had lived through, it felt as
if our infrastructure, body and spirit, had to be rebuilt from
scratch. Even our automatic responses had to be restarted,
retrained, and reimagined. The blues are constantly reborn.

Not long after Stella's first Thanksgiving without her
father, she cornered me in the kitchen after school. The determined look on her face told me that another session in
our protracted sugar negotiation was about to commence.
After five years of this debate, I was ready for her. She said,
"Mommy, is Santa Claus real?" Oh crap, did not see that
coming. There it was . . . *the* question. She'd already lost her
daddy; the last thing I wanted to do was kill off Santa Claus,
too. This kid could not catch a break. Nor, it seemed, could
I—without John, my partner in fielding the tough questions, all I had to go on was instinct and fear.

I asked her, "How would you feel if I said yes, he is
real?" And my five-year-old replied, "I would know that I
couldn't trust you anymore about anything because you
don't trust me with the truth." So I sat down on the kitchen
floor, took her hands, and pulled her down to face me, then
I said, "Nope. Santa Claus is not real." We both welled up
with tears; she put her head in my lap and I folded over to
cover her with my body. Together, we grieved for Santa—we
were getting pretty damn good at it by then. When we loos-
ened our origami hugs to look at each other again, I said,
"I'm so sorry, Stella. So sorry Santa was never real." And she
said, "Well, at least Dad was."

Our first Christmas without John was bearing down on

us. I could feel the dread accumulating all around me. Talk about going through the motions. I could not believe the world was actually going to have Christmas without John. Really? It's still on? Yet there we were: the grieving widow and the self-proclaimed half-orphan.

This fact was not lost on extended family, friends, and fans. All of whom seemed, at the time, to be of the opinion that if we could just power our way through the Christmas grind, the prize of a shiny new year awaited us. The traditional "Happy Holidays" greeting was supplanted by a strange holiday chorus that went something like, "*Oh my God!* Aren't you glad 2003 is going to be over? What a horrible year for your family." The first time I heard someone say what was to become a 2003 instant holiday standard, it was met by my blank stare and an awkward moment of silence. Turns out that this question was not meant to be rhetorical; the well-meaning well-wishers wanted some kind of validation of their theory.

Usually, I can sense a conversation I don't want to be in even before it starts. Years of BSing my way through Catholic school on charm (matter of opinion) and Cliffs Notes (matter of fact) had heightened my "this could be trouble" detector to superhero level. Just call me The Avoidinator. By fifth grade, I could read a nun's face on the approach and have the appropriate excuse ready instantly, as if it were scripted. Clues like an overexcited intake of breath before speaking or too much white showing around the irises accompanied by a disapproving tongue cluck had always been enough to raise my bat shields. My avoidance techniques became instantaneous and entertaining (to me, at least), as I

doled out a seemingly endless supply of sugarcoated deception pellets, like a Pez dispenser with my head on it.

However, in the face of this new reality, commiserating
over the first holiday season without John, my skills let me
down. That our whole family should be relieved that this
fucked-up year was coming to an end seemed to be obvious to everyone but me. I was caught by surprise every time.
My "rut-ro detector" was disabled by the onslaught of general agreement. When called upon to agree with someone's
assessment of the end of the year from hell, relief I should
naturally be feeling, I would panic. Then I would employ
my halfhearted headshake, neither "yes" nor "no," just a
bobble-headed, widowy nod that I had recently adopted.
It was one of the many techniques the bereft version of me
would have to develop in the next few years to simply exist
in the world. The dodge always satisfied whoever was doing
the asking, but no matter how polite they were, to me the
exchange always felt like a constipated talk show interview. I
simply could not engage anyone about it.

The concept of throwing out the whole year just did not
sit right with me. And it pissed me off. Call me crazy, but it
was the last year Stella, Carly, Tyler, and Jason had a father,
and the last year I was a wife—2003 had been one-fifth of
Stella's life, for God's sake. It was a year full of living and
loving, and we all will forever be racking our brains to recall
every tiny moment and fleeting memory from it for the rest
of our lives.

John was happy and at his best. He was thrilled to be
working and was having a ball at Disney. All of his kids were
growing and exploring the world in ways that blew his mind

every day. He shared their excitement and relished every moment he could be with them on their journeys. We all loved 2003 and we lived the hell out of it. The sadness that permeated the last few months of it could never diminish how precious that year was and will be for us. Forever.

When you are grieving alongside your young child, there's a fine line that you have to tread between authenticity and self-indulgence. If that means that you, as an adult, need to eat it for a couple of hours until your kid goes to bed before wailing your eyes out into your pillow, then so be it. Your child needs to know that it's okay to talk to you and that doing so is not going to set you off.

There was a time early on when Stella asked me a question about John, and I would launch into a monologue about him and his philosophies and how his legacy would endure, just going on and on. Meanwhile, her question had been something like "What was his favorite color?" I realized that I was, inadvertently, taking the opportunity to have a whole "get in touch" session with my daughter, when her question simply warranted a one-word answer. My first instinct was to blather on to her the way I was blathering on to myself in my head. I caught myself almost immediately and trained myself to always take an imperceptible pause before speaking. I promised to answer her questions as honestly and succinctly as I could. Existential ponderings on my part were to be kept in my own head.

chapter 22

Teaspoon of Jupiter

It's hard to describe those first few weeks following John's death. It was as if gravity had multiplied. I seemed to be held to the Earth more profoundly than those with less weighty psychic loads. It was not so much a matter of the depth of despair as it was the density of it. My every molecule was exponentially heavier. A teaspoon of Jupiter.

Forced by the clock and expectation to test the parameters of my comfort zone, ticking off tasks and fending off the paralyzing effects of grief, I walked through each day with my leash still firmly held by the real me who was cowering beneath the blankets, unable and unwilling to tempt fate and physics. I could hardly bear the impossible hours of separation from myself. I moved as if submerged, trying to ignore the inevitable twinge signaling the inescapable tug of the yo-yo string and my dutiful return to my new reality. The end of another day, resigned, I would crawl into my bed and into my truth, relieved and horrified to be reunited with myself.

The first time I went back to my routine, to what I was doing the day before my husband died, I immediately understood the concept of "the black veil." Although for me, it was more like seeing the world through grief-colored glasses, definitely more blue than black. My frame of reference for everything from the mundane to the sublime was skewed. Possibly sharpened. Definitely changed. Forever. My perception of the world, as I peered from behind the imaginary veil, made me feel separate. Not just separate from other people, but from the former me I would never be able to get back to.

The world had split into "John" and "After John." I would have pangs of disgust for myself—embarrassment, really—when I would flash back to a moment of frustration or sadness prior to John's death. I started to really beat myself up about the time wasted and energy spent over petty disappointments and everyday aggravations. What the hell was I crying about then? The *widow* me began judging the *wife* me with exasperated derision.

The week before John died, I remember being so bummed out about taking Stella to her first day of kindergarten. I was crying to him in the kitchen about how much I would miss her. My God, now I know what missing really is. That same week, I remember being pissed off when I found out that John was scheduled do Ellen DeGeneres's show on September 18, our anniversary. And then: our anniversary rolls around, John's been gone for seven days, and I'm lying flat on the kitchen floor in the dark, devastated and fantasizing about how beautiful it would've been to pick out his tie and help him think up entertaining anecdotes for Ellen and her audience. My God, what a joy that would have been, to have him for another week. Just to have him.

Increasingly hypercritical of my former self, I would struggle to remember what made me sad before John died, and it would not only pale in comparison to my new circumstances but it would exacerbate my grief to know I had wasted time. I would think, *This is what passed for a problem in those days?* You know, the good old days—a week ago, a day ago, an hour ago—back when I wasn't a widow, before the doctor opened his mouth and said the words that changed my life, and Stella's, forever.

There seems to be a scale of tragedy—it's something we're always aware of subconsciously. Some tragedies put a crimp in your day; others destroy all life as you know it. But until you're at the epicenter of your own life-changing drama, you may lack the ability to put things in perspective. It has less to do with the degree of devastation ("My tragedy can kick your tragedy's ass!") than it has to do with proximity.

John was fond of Charlie Chaplin's point of view on "point of view": Drama is life in a close-up, comedy is life in a long shot. Distance dictates your perspective. Perspective is perception. If you see your neighbor slip on his kid's roller-skate and face-plant on the lawn across the street, it's comedy. When it's you—your slip, your fall, in all of its awkward cartilage-crunching glory—it's drama.

The danger in judging yourself harshly for your pre-widowhood blindness comes when you start unfairly judging other people. For some, a tsunami halfway around the world is a just blip on their radar. But if their bathtub overflows, they describe it as a "disaster area." One mitigating factor that dictates perception of tragedy is proximity: When the devastation is in your own backyard, it is huge to you. But a natural disaster on the other side of the globe probably registers lower on your personal scale of tragedy if you are not directly affected by it. Proximity, whether it's physical closeness or emotional attachment, seems to determine the impact a tragedy has on your life.

Our family's very, very intimate tragedy of losing John— our father, brother, husband, friend—was shared by thousands and thousands of people who had never met him. The distance was bridged. This was due less to the power of the media than to the power of John the man. He was, in a word, knowable. It was always stunning to me that the intensity and diversity of his ebullient, serious, goofy, romantic personality that was spent on us here at home was seemingly inexhaustible. Not to say, by any means, that the outer circle, outside of his family and friends, got the whole picture. But when I think about how much he gave away to the public . . . a lesser guy wouldn't have had any of his personality left to bring back home with him at the end of the day.

John did not hold back. Not his talent. Not his love. Not his appreciation. People felt John's passing so deeply not just because he was in their home by way of the living room television set. So many of the people with whom I've spoken or who have written to me clearly pictured him sitting on their living room couch as well. He inadvertently made himself part of their family. And the guy you saw on TV was very much the real guy. When people say to me, "I loved your husband," I always say, "He loved you, too."

I've learned to become very accepting of people's expressions of the grief they feel. I had to really dig down to a selfless place inside of me. And I had to do it fast. As private as losing my husband obviously was, the world did not have time to wait for me to recover my public face. The power of John's life and talent brought his loss very close to home for a lot of folks. It's no wonder that, for so many people, losing John Ritter ranked high on the scale of tragedy for them. And instead of resenting them for presuming to have known my husband, I had to accept that this is exactly what John was doing all those years. He was drawing people close by plucking "the golden thread that runs through all of us," as he used to say.

Using comedy to express the commonality of the human condition was his life's work. Its enduring effect on the world at large should have been no surprise to me. But I am still constantly surprised and deeply heartened by the personal bond people feel with John. As empathetic as we are— or strive to be—it is still a miracle, a dangerous feat of faith, to truly feel someone else's pain. If we could actually feel each other's sorrow the way the true sufferer experiences it, the world would stop moving altogether. It is a solitary experience that I was taught to believe is, ultimately, beneficial. Pain and grief are not unlike a fever that burn for a reason: to purge and purify your body. But I have a hard time with this idea; I have never fully bought into the concept. To me, the expression "That which does not kill you makes you stronger," should always be followed by "if not wary, reclusive, and unduly suspicious."

I grew up with the concept of purgatory. Even after the Vatican II Council of Bishops in 1965 all but obliterated the notion, it was still a staple of my spiritual diet. Apparently, we Catholics in Cincinnati did not get the message right away—my parents were undeterred by the wave of changes washing over the Church. They had been raised to accept the conditions laid out in this afterlife escrow agreement. Were they really supposed to accept that all credit accrued by indulgences, paid or prayed, was now wiped away along with the debt?

When I was growing up, every scraped knee, social disappointment, and menstrual cramp was "offered up for the souls in purgatory," the tacit agreement of Catholic karma being: you scratch my sins, I'll scratch yours. Quid pro quo. It was as if your grandma was in an afterlife halfway house and got to move out early because of *your* "good behavior." Your good behavior being the ability to suffer stoically with the knowledge that doing so will spring Grandma before her sentence is up.

Even though I, along with most of the Catholic Church, have abandoned the notion of purgatory, the general concept is inexorably etched in my brain. It was natural—heck, unavoidable—that I would seek (however unconsciously) a meaning, an upside, if you will (I will if you will), to the grief we were suffering through when John died.

When Stella went back to school four days after the funeral, it was class picture day. Oh boy. When her little picture packet arrived a couple of weeks later, I just sat down on the kitchen floor and stared into her eyes on the 8 x 10. She had this brave, crooked grin. She was really trying to be a five-year-old on picture day at her brand-new school. But the world as she knew it was shattered. The other children in her class weren't even worried about losing their first tooth yet, and my little girl was being asked to endure losing her daddy. I couldn't then, and won't ever be able to, assuage the pain she feels and that I feel for her by assigning a positive effect to her loss.

My parents died when I was very young. And I was so thoroughly preconditioned to just endure with the confidence that I would be rightfully rewarded for my earthly suffering that I did not question the logic of the deal. I was willing, in terms of my parents, to entertain the "suffering is good" theory as it pertained to me and my grief. But twenty years later when I lost my husband, it just didn't stick. I wasn't buying it in relation to my little girl.

When Stella and I talked about our feelings in those first few months, we did so with a freedom and honesty that I had not allowed myself before. When my parents died, although I was questioning the tenets of my religion at the time, I reverted to the dogma of my upbringing. Any question that was preanswered for me was greatly appreciated. But when John died, even though it would've been expedient to pass on the tradition of "this will all make sense in the afterlife, where you will be compensated for your tears," I couldn't do it.

Over the years, I have come to realize that your character isn't formed by suffering. It doesn't make you a better person. It's not a blessing, in disguise or otherwise. I understand why that belief is sincerely and reverently held: it makes our own misery easier to tolerate. "Suffering is ultimately good" also has the added benefit of affording a kind of justification for turning a blind eye to others' pain. If the upshot of all this agony is an upgrade either here on Earth or beyond, then why should we strive to alleviate suffering, either physical or emotional, for anyone? That would just deprive them of the chance to burnish their soul to perfection by way of the turmoil tumbler.

In my experience, character is formed not because of, but *in spite* of, suffering. How we deal with, and encourage our kids to deal with, the inevitability of heartache is the framework on which personhood is built. And no matter how I was programmed or what words I was expected to say, I could only share with my daughter what was truly in my heart.

Suffering happens; our reaction to it is the only thing over which we have control. I want Stella to know that although we experience grief, it does not define us. It neither diminishes nor elevates our value as human beings. Suffering has worth only in that it informs and enriches the depth and quality of our empathy. And empathy is the purest way to experience our connection to the rest of the world and to confirm for ourselves that we aren't alone. Hmm . . . seems like we're back to "suffering is good." Fine. But I'm still not buying that it earns the dearly departed one-way frequent-flyer miles from purgatory to heaven.

chapter 23

A Grief History of Time

When I was a panelist on the revamped version of *I've Got a Secret*, I met dozens and dozens of interesting contestants with wild stories to tell about their esoteric lifestyles and careers and world records. The most fascinating to me, besides the freaking genius who invented Spanx (bless you, lady), was the woman who held the record for holding her breath underwater. She was famous for diving deeper and staying down longer without oxygen tanks than any other human being on record. Where was this lady when I was twenty-five and filming thirty feet down in The Living Seas exhibit at Epcot Center? I could have used a good swim/life coach when I was thrashing around in *Splash, Too*. I don't know if this real-life mermaid had stretched out her lungs, slowed down her heartbeat, or perfected some sort of underwater meditation that overrode the primal response of panic that results from lack of air. She must have practiced for years, building her endurance and adding about half a second every day, pushing herself until she reached her goal.

It reminded me of an amazingly disturbing science segment I watched on *That's Incredible* when I was in high school. (Clearly, this was before the Discovery Channel; getting your science from John Davidson, Fran Tarkington, and Cathy Lee Crosby was risky at best, but always entertaining.) A fairly credible-looking scientist-type held a tiny white mouse over a glass beaker of what was described as "liquid oxygen." The helpless little guy was dropped into the beaker and held "underwater" with what appeared to be a tongue depressor. He immediately freaked out, frantically paddling and twisting in an attempt to wriggle free. When the mouse finally gave up his panicked acrobatics, exhausted, he opened his mouth and took a breath of "water." Actually, he was breathing superoxygenated fluorocarbon. But it was incredible (literally) to see him completely submerged—not drowning, not flailing, just getting used to the idea.

For me, at the beginning, grieving was a lot like learning to breathe liquid oxygen. I had to instantly figure out how to simultaneously mourn, mother, and live. There was no time to prepare: No practice dives into the world of widowhood to help me build up a tolerance to my new situation. No time to train myself not to freak out; I was totally submerged like my little mouse friend. In over my head, I was forced to wrap my tiny brain around the fact that nothing was ever going to be the same. Ever. I was breathing water. And I was still alive.

Grieving a loss not only requires that you begin experiencing the world alone but that you come to grips with the fact that your loved one can never experience it again. This realization is paralyzing. I now understand the impulse in some traditions to regard everything a wife does after her husband passes away as immodest. Everything. In some cultures, just surviving, just being alive, is an affront to the dearly departed. From time immemorial, widows have been encouraged and expected to brick themselves up in their husbands' pyramids or fling themselves onto the funeral pyre.

Obviously, I don't agree with this ideology and, intellectually, I absolutely reject it. But intellectual objectivity aside, after you lose your partner, there is a pervasive patina of guilt that subtly creeps into your daily life. In some cultures around the world, women still observe the ancient custom of cutting their hair as a visible symbol of mourning—the idea being that once your husband is gone from this Earth, your hair, your femininity, your sexuality should be exorcised from your being. So widows chop off their hair to avoid having their crowning freaking glory glimpsed by another man. Shearing your hair, tearing down the curtains in your house, rending your clothing—all of these traditions express a rip in the fabric of your being, the end of life as you know it. I get that. I felt it.

The morning of John's funeral, I sat in front of the mirror with a pair of scissors in my hand. I eyed my long locks, which looked conspicuously brash to me. My hair seemed as if it belonged to the pre-widow me. Incongruous, and the red definitely clashed with my blues. I cut into the ends, half-expecting to feel the blades; I could no longer distinguish which parts of me were alive and which parts were dead. I didn't know what I was supposed to feel at that point. After wrestling with the idea for a while, I successfully fought the urge to shear myself. Instead I just ended up giving myself a shitty haircut. Then, as much as I would rather have been curled up in the fetal position sobbing my brains out, I fought gravity, remained upright, and dragged a burning hot flat iron through my hair. I went through the motions. My morning ritual. My *mourning* ritual. I looked in the mirror again, and the scissors-wielding maniac had transformed into just me, doing my hair, for my husband, one last time.

In May of 2004, I was working on *Life on a Stick* for the Fox network, and I was invited to attend the finale of season three of *American Idol*. I was an unabashed fan of *Idol*, but the expectation that I would plug our show also made it a work thing. I had to go. The idea of yucking it up on the press line did feel a little odd. It also felt a little wonky to be showing up alone. I was relieved when my angel of a friend, Holly Robinson Pete, and her husband, Rodney, told me that they were attending and would look after me. True to their word they hung by my side for the entire event. Especially impressive was Rodney—an NFL quarterback for sixteen years—who showed his flexibility by running interference for the Widow Ritter all night.

Not until I read the paper the next day did I realize that I had been "controversial." The caption under the picture of my arrival sent me scurrying to my computer. "Widow weeds?" I was already out of my "widow weeds"? Wikipedia informed me that it was a Victorian term for the traditional black dress worn for a year and a day. It was not my intention to raise eyebrows; I really had no idea how genuinely offended some folks would be. When I walked my red head down the red carpet in my red dress, I did it for John. I guess I couldn't expect anyone to appreciate that fact.

The first time John had ever actually seen the inside of my closet, he stood incredulous, shaking his head and counting my little black dresses. He thought it was ridiculous that a girl my age would wear nothing but black. I know: slimming, classic, always appropriate black. But he just couldn't see it. He said, "Honey, I'm fourteen years older than you are; chances are, you'll have plenty of time to wear black way down the road." My response to his particular brand of dark humor was predictable and he had, early on, learned to tense his arm in anticipation. A quick punch to his bicep would always accompany my plea, "John, pleeease don't joke about that kind of stuff."

My preference for subtle tones was a bewildering phenomenon to John, who was—to put it mildly—a fan of colorful clothes, the brighter the better. This was not a man who hesitated to don any pigment of the imagination. Every once in a while, he would bounce down the stairs on his way out the door, and I would just bite my tongue and smile at his ensemble. More than once, when I would look askance at one of his outfits, he would claim that he had felt sorry for a forlorn shirt or sweater that he hadn't worn in a while. "I see this orange vest looking at me hopefully every day, and this morning I just said to it, 'Today's your day, buddy, come on!'" I kid you not.

John didn't care what anyone thought of his wardrobe.

But he would occasionally ask Stella what she thought of a particular outfit. She would just glance up from the *Teletubbies* to see her father sporting the same color scheme as the Furry Fab Four and give him an approving thumbs-up. This colorful quirk of his seemed to be an overflowing of who he was on the inside. Even his clothes were entertaining. After he died, these shirts and ties and jackets—from the sedate to the elegant to the bizarre—became treasures.

The week after the funeral, all of my family and my out-of-state friends had returned to the Midwest and to points beyond, and Stella had started back at school. I was alone in our house. I dreaded what was waiting for me. I knew of widows who were five, ten, fifteen years out, and had never touched their husband's clothes. Too real. I totally got it. I knew it was a duty left only to me. And if I didn't throw myself into it immediately, it would never happen.

When John did the movie version of the Broadway play *Noises Off,* he had to perform an enormous stunt—a full-on tumble down a staircase. It was clearly dangerous, but John wanted to do it himself. When it came time for John to throw himself down the stairs, people began to gather on the set. Even though, through the years, we all saw Jack Tripper flip over couches, spin out of hammocks, trip, fall, bash his head (once, actually knocking himself out for a moment), this was a little scarier. This is what stuntmen are for. But nooooo . . . John donned his elbow and knee pads and threw himself down the long wooden staircase. When the director yelled "Cut," it took John a moment to untangle himself from his position at the bottom of the stairs. Most human beings in that situation would have called for a break to gather their wits and have their bruises tended, but John said, "Just get me back up to the landing. I want to do it again now." And, by God, he did. He took full advantage of the fact that his body was in shock. This physical comedy version of "getting back up on the horse" has become, for me, a parable about survival. My version of throwing myself down the stairs a second time, while still in a daze, was diving headlong into the impossibly painful task of divvying up John's possessions.

After a few weeks, I actually allowed myself to start driving all the way back home after dropping Stella off at school (instead of sitting on the side of the road in my car with John's Dodger cap pulled down over my eyes). On those caffeine-fueled mornings, I would burst through my kitchen door, throw my keys on the counter, and walk straight upstairs and into John's closet, where I would be surrounded by his stuff. Dozens of jackets and suits, at least half of it wardrobe from his TV shows and movies. He had more Hawaiian shirts than most Honolulu gift shops. Hilo Hattie's had nothing on John.

I would grab a handful of hangers and begin separating the clothing. I knew what a comfort it would be for John's friends and family to have something physical to hold on to. A little something. A memento. John was very, very sentimental about clothes. And everyone knew that if they admired something John was wearing, he would give it to them. If it was something essential, it would arrive in the mail to you in about a week; if it could be removed without exposing him to indecency charges, it would be yours immediately.

John would always take his boys into his closet and load them up with jackets and shirts. It was always the same routine: "I thought you might like this since, apparently, I've been working out too hard and have become too muscular to fit into this shirt." Riiiiight.

His daughter Carly and I loved wearing John's sweaters and shirts. His clothes were roomy, worn-in, and Dad-riffic. With his blessing, all of us raided his closet on a regular basis. Now there was an abundance of clothes and an absence of Dad. It was overwhelmingly sad to take each piece off the hanger, fold it, and assign it a destination. But most important was assigning a pile for each kid. I saved a lot for Stella. I didn't think it was appropriate to involve her, at her age, in this process. But I knew that one day she would want to wrap John's sweaters around her if she couldn't have his arms.

This task was not like folding the laundry. Nor was it a matter of wistful reminiscing. This game of widow's solitaire, sorting and assigning each item to its pile, was not played to pass the time, but to stop it. As I look back on it now, I think it served to slow down the breakneck speed at which my world was changing. Every item had its own story. There were pieces from every movie and television show and play that John had ever done. These were gifts, mind you, he hadn't pinched them. There were also souvenirs from adventures we had shared with each other and with our kids.

Then there were the ties. So many ties. Ties from every era. Skinny, wide, short, long—even bolo ties, to go with his Western-style tuxedo, obviously—and for the man who has everything tie-wise, hand-painted ones. (Hand-painted by me, of course.) I got better at it as the years went on. I started out just drawing on silk ties with Sharpies. Then I advanced to painting on them and writing sassy messages on the backs. He loved them and embraced their evolution with the same grace and gratitude with which he ate my attempts at cooking. The funny thing about the ties is: he actually wore them, in public, a lot. He didn't care how funky they looked; he would wear them on television and to important functions, and when people would ask him about them, he would say, "It's a *Yasbeck*."

The first box of John's belongings that I actually had the nerve to send was to my nephew Mark. He was serving with the 101st Airborne in Iraq at the time, and he had written to us, saying that he and his fellow soldiers were in dire need of socks. They wore layers of them and walked so much that the ones they had been issued were threadbare and causing painful blisters. Not only were the blisters painful, but Mark once pulled on his army-issue socks and shoved his foot into a boot, only to feel the decidedly new sensation of a scorpion sting. He pulled out his foot to see a baby scorpion still clinging to the sole of his sock. I don't know if wearing three layers would have made a difference, but why not help the kid hedge his bets. I balled up about three dozen pairs of white sweat socks and put them in a cardboard box along with John's collection of *Mad* magazines. John would have loved the image of all those freshly socked, twentysomething soldiers earnestly trying to decipher the 1980s references in *Mad* and glean what little humor they could from parodies of TV shows they had never heard of.

Not all of the athletic socks made their way into the box. There was a particular pair of white tube socks with two green stripes that caught my eye. One morning around the beginning of *8 Simple Rules,* John was walking out the door on the way to Starbucks in an electric blue Hawaiian shirt, red gym shorts, Birkenstocks, and those striped knee socks. This time, I could not hold my tongue. When he kissed me good-bye, I gave him the once-over and said as sweetly as I could, "*Really,* John?" Borrowing from a Mary J. Blige MTV interview that had riveted us the night before, he turned his baseball cap to the side and said, "I dress for my peeps."

Sitting on the floor of John's closet I folded my treasures and put them to the side. The white tube socks with green stripes were not going anywhere. When someone is gone forever, little things that formerly meant nothing become everything. They are often the catalyst for a sense memory so substantial, so genuine, that you feel transported. Like Alice wondering what would happen if she opened this little door, or drank from that bottle marked DRINK ME. Mourning is a Wonderland of sorts. You certainly never know where the day will take you. You've clearly fallen down a rabbit hole, or slipped through some kind of time-space wormhole. Any object, picture, scent, taste, or sound can evoke a memory so real that it's disorienting.

Letting go of John's things was necessary, heartbreaking, and draining. At some point every day, my wave of Starbucks-induced energy would ebb—and triple nonfat whatever aside, I would inevitably fall asleep, exhausted, on a pile of clothes. That walk-in closet and its painfully evocative contents became my world. The intimate nature of grief is isolating; you do feel cut off from other people, from the nongrieving majority. There was a certain comfort in knowing that this ritual had been performed by the bereft for millennia. The very fact that others had gone down this road before heartened me. The concept of "going it alone" seemed doable when I came to embrace the reality that I really wasn't alone at all.

The feeling reminded me of winters in Cincinnati, when the snow would fall all night and completely change the landscape by morning. You knew that the snow wasn't just in your yard, but in your neighbors' yards, down the street, all over the city—it was everywhere at the same time. Everyone was awake early, running their cars in hopes of warming them up a degree or two before driving off. The idea was to get it, if not toasty, to a temperature survivable by humans—or by Midwesterners, at least. Everyone was scraping their windshields and Ohio-swearing ("Jeezus Pete" and "Shitski!") while fruitlessly breathing hot air into their frozen gloves. Knowing that this cluster-frost was a shared experience didn't lessen the effort required to shovel your own driveway. But there was something about the knowledge that you weren't alone that went a long way toward warming your heart, if not your front seat.

For me, the fact that other widows had weathered the storm meant that I had a chance of surviving, surviving John.

chapter 24

From the Heart

Don't accept that what's happening is just a case of others suffering
Or you'll find that you're joining in the Turning Away
—PINK FLOYD

John's autograph was, most times, preceded by the words "with love and laughter." Laughter is the part that everyone who knew John and loved his work shared. And I'm here to tell you that, yes, he did love, in a big way—his family, his friends, and all of his fellow travelers in life.

The unexpected aspect of John's legacy has to do with the love people still feel for him. When John died, it wasn't just his family and friends who were stunned. People all over the world wanted to know why we had to lose John. When the answer came back, "We didn't," a major shift took place in the way people think about aortic disease.

For years and years, scientists, doctors, surgeons, and policy makers have been hard at work to bring this devastating condition, its genetic component, and correct diagnosis and treatment to light. It seems like everyone knows of someone who has died from an undiagnosed aortic aneurysm. But only when it impacts your own family can you feel the full effect. The love and affection that people felt and still feel for John, and the impact of losing him, have served to awaken the consciousness of the public and the medical community alike. His philosophy of life was about plucking that golden thread of humanity that connects us all. Not only did he employ his gifts to make his audience laugh, but also to see. John understood and embraced the responsibility of using his notoriety to bring awareness and focus to innumerable worthy causes. Knowing John the way I did made my mission clear.

Information is power. And nothing renders you as powerless as losing a loved one to something you don't understand. When John died, Stella wanted answers right away. After the crush and the disorienting blur of the first day, she asked me, "Did Daddy die of a broken heart?" What I wanted to say was, "No, sweetheart, Daddy didn't die of a broken heart, but I feel like I might." Instead I explained, the best I could at the time, that it was something near his heart that broke. I got out crayons and paper and drew the basics of what I knew for her. Then she worked on a copy for herself: an anatomical heart and aorta. She asked me to write on her drawing: "The aorta is close to our heart."

Stella wasn't the only one who was confused about the cause of John's death. Most of the public thinks cardiovascular means "heart-related." And make no mistake, it is clearly perceived and received as *cardio*-vascular. Thanks to the much-maligned pharmaceutical companies, we are made to think about our heart, and the potential of heart disease, literally every day. Ads on TV and in magazines ask us to consider our eating habits, our family history, our blood pressure and cholesterol, to determine what medication we may need. But aorta-wise: nada, no awareness. Didn't know I had one. Don't know where it is.

Most of the articles I read and television reports I saw when John died implied that it had been a random tragedy, as if a freaking satellite fell out of the sky and landed on him. Many even took the fact that the tear in his aorta was *undetected* and stretched reality to report that it was *undetectable*. It wasn't just the tabloids, major newspapers and network news shows were reporting that he had died of an "undetectable heart defect." Not only is aortic dissection *not* undetectable, but the aorta is not even part of the heart. Poetically referred to as "The Tree of Life" and "The River Nile of Human Anatomy," the aorta is the largest artery in our body, running the length of our torso. Blood from the heart is pumped through the aortic valve into the beginning of the aorta, where it is then channeled and delivered to your entire body. A tear in its wall means death.

The dissection is the shearing away of an inner wall of the aorta, most likely caused by an aneurysm or dilation of this section. Like a weakening in an automobile tire or a garden hose, these aneurysms gradually expand to a dangerous size. With the correct imaging, they can absolutely be seen before they have reached destructive proportions. When John died, the press's overwhelming impetus to stress the suddenness and drama of his passing diverted our attention from the science. By using the words "undetectable" and "heart," they were 0 for 2. And we were all still in the dark. It would take John's extended family of fans and friends to shine a light on this disease.

Against everyone's well-intentioned advice, I began to open the big boxes of mail that were stacked on my kitchen floor. They had begun to accumulate just days after John died, finding their way to me through publicists and agents and studios. Up until then, I had not had the heart to read the condolence letters and sympathy cards that had been delivered to me in the previous month.

Tearing open that first box and seeing, for the first time, the outpouring of love from John's fans took my breath away. Some were store-bought cards signed by entire families. Some were homemade cards with stickers of Clifford on them. Many had personal stories of what John's talent and humor had contributed to their lives. The sheer volume, coupled with the intense heartfelt sadness of the public, was overwhelming. But more unexpected still, was a growing pile of mail I began to sort out from the rest. Interspersed with messages of support and sympathy, were a couple dozen letters from people telling a different story about aortic dissection—personal stories of misdiagnosis, genetic links, and most important, survival.

Shortly after reading some of these letters, I was given an amazing article by Kevin Helliker and Tom Burton from the *Wall Street Journal*. Things I had suspected, things I feared, were all there in black and white. That article was one of ten articles on aortic dissection, and the writers went on to win the Pulitzer Prize for explanatory reporting for the series. I began to contact the surgeons and scientists and to research the studies that had been referenced. I was finally getting a true picture of the nature of this beast.

In many ways, it would have been easier to accept the media's general misinterpretation about John's death and aortic dissection. Believing that he was taken from us by an invisible, unstoppable monster is horrible enough. Realizing that we were ambushed by an insidious slow-growing gremlin is infuriating. The correct imaging would have detected the aneurysm; if we had caught this thing in just the right light, it would have been exposed. We never got a chance to engage it in battle. There are armies of dedicated surgeons and scientists equipped and ready to do just that. I was determined to do anything I could to make sure aortic dissection was brought out into the bright light of day, so it couldn't sneak up on anyone else. I knew there were families headed for the same fate as ours and I couldn't waste time. First, the vulnerable aneurysms have to be detected. These undetected aneurysms were time bombs, ticking away in parents, brothers, sisters, children; I felt compelled to give people the tools to defuse them.

Walking up to the podium to address a room full of cardiovascular surgeons for the first time, I was all too aware of my own heart: somehow broken to bits and pounding full throttle in my chest at the same time. Maybe it was too soon to jump into the fray. It hadn't even been a year since we had lost John. I was understandably still reeling from the shock of my husband succumbing to something that wasn't just "not on *my* radar," but that was clearly not on the doctors' radar the night he died.

As nerve-rattling as this speech would be, it was a relief to be in a room filled with people who were as preoccupied with all things aortic as I was. I didn't have to hide my obsession. I was among my people. I finally understood the appeal of a *Star Trek* convention. The increased awareness of aortic disease that was brought about by John's death is a gift, a blessing to the thousands and thousands of people who are more likely to be diagnosed correctly and saved.

The reason the public is "heart-smart" and "aorta-ignorant" is because as of now, there is no one-a-day, aneurysm-shrinking, dissection-mending pill (with plenty of *x*'s and *z*'s in its name, as in "Ask your doctor if Zzzaortex is right for you"). We are not going to be inundated any time soon by cool computer graphics of bicuspid valves and aortic aches during the commercial breaks of *Monday Night Football*. The drug companies don't feel compelled to make aortic aneurysm and dissection water-cooler conversation. As of now, there is no money in it for them.

Every day since having my own consciousness raised regarding aortic aneurysm and dissection, I have passed on information in ways large and small to the public regarding this disease. I know that John's death and the awareness that it has brought to aortic dissection has already saved lives. Occasionally, I will hear from a family telling me that a family member was saved because of John's sacrifice. I never felt comfortable with that word—"sacrifice"—until a rabbi friend of mine explained that in Hebrew the word for sacrifice and gift are the same. John gave the gift of his talent freely to the world. And the gift of his love to his family and friends is legendary and enduring. I don't think anyone could have foreseen the gift of life that he would give to his brother, Tommy, years after his own passing.

In 2003, after John died, his relatives were scanned and their thoracic aortic diameter measured to make sure that they were in the normal range. In 2007, Tommy suffered a minor stroke. By that time, all of John's kids and Tom were participating in a study at the University of Texas, headed by Dr. Dianna Milewicz. Dianna had become my friend and my mentor, catching me up (as well as a layperson can be caught up) on the science of aortic dissection and the genes responsible for putting individuals at risk. Her groundbreaking work was shedding light on the mystery of Familial Aortic Aneurysm and Dissection. I called her to make her aware of Tommy's stroke and she made sure that I understood that this was a serious development. Her latest work had led her to some very strong connections between brain and aortic aneurysms. She urged me to get Tommy rescanned and his aorta measured again, in case it had become aneurismal.

Tommy's new imaging showed an aneurysm in the same place as the one that had killed his brother, his ascending aorta. In December 2007, Tommy's aorta was repaired in a twelve-hour open chest surgery by Dr. Craig Miller at Stanford University. His aneurysm had grown so large that had it not been detected he would not have lived to see the New Year. John had given the gift of life to his brother.

It is believed now that John and Tom's father, Tex, most likely died of an aortic dissection rather the heart attack reported at the time. Our family knows the risk all too well.

I want to make sure that people have the correct information about symptoms and about the genetic connection so that they can advocate for themselves even in their doctor's office. I started the John Ritter Foundation for Aortic Health to raise public and professional awareness through research and education because I want more people aware, observed, treated, fixed—and alive.

I know for sure that the awareness "tipping point" for any disease comes when information is shared in both directions. When scientists and clinicians come to an agreement on how to move forward on a disease, language becomes more precise and readily available to all of us. I want the public to be empowered with the facts. A multispecialty aortic disease guideline has recently been published. It focuses on diagnosis and treatment of acute aortic dissection, as well as emerging knowledge in the area of familial tendencies and genetic mutations that lead to the development of thoracic aortic aneurysms and dissections.

Working so closely with the doctors, scientists, and fellow activists who have made this breakthrough a reality, has changed my view of medicine. I know that we, the public, can understand and participate in our own health care if we are armed with the correct information. The esoteric language of medicine and genetics that typically bounces around in the higher echelon of medical science will not trickle down to us without our asking. In an effort to make sure this life-saving information in the guidelines finds its way to everyone, our family has gladly gifted John's name to an accessible and understandable version of the guidelines.

Ritter Rules

Ritter Rules are life-saving reminders to recognize, treat, and prevent thoracic aortic dissection.

URGENCY: Thoracic aortic dissection is a medical emergency. The death rate increases 1 percent every hour the diagnosis and surgical repair are delayed.

PAIN: Severe pain is the #1 symptom. Seek immediate emergency medical care for a sudden onset of severe pain in the chest, stomach, back, or neck. The pain is likely to be sharp, tearing, ripping, moving, or so unlike any pain you have ever had that you feel something is very wrong.

MISDIAGNOSIS: Aortic dissection can mimic a heart attack. Heart attacks are far more common than aortic dissection. But if a heart attack or other important diagnosis is not clearly and quickly established, then aortic dissection should be quickly considered and ruled out, particularly if a patient has a family history or features of a genetic syndrome that predisposes the patient to an aortic aneurysm or dissection.

IMAGING: Get the right scan to rule out aortic dissection. Only three types of imaging studies can identify aortic aneurysms and dissections: CT, MRI, and transesophageal echocardiogram. A chest X-ray or EKG cannot rule out aortic dissection.

RISK FACTOR: Aortic dissections are often proceeded by an enlargement of the first part of the aorta where it comes out of the heart, called an aortic aneurysm. If you have an aneurysm, you are at an increased risk for an aortic dissection.

RISK FACTOR: A personal or family history of thoracic disease puts you at risk. If you or a family member is living with an aneurysm or if you have a family member who has had an aortic dissection, you are at an increased risk for thoracic aortic dissection. You and your other family members should be evaluated to determine if a predisposition for aortic aneurysm and dissection runs in the family.

RISK FACTOR: Certain genetic syndromes put you at risk. These genetic syndromes greatly increase your risk for thoracic aortic disease and a potentially fatal aortic dissection: Marfan syndrome, Loeys-Dietz syndrome, Turner syndrome, and vascular Ehlers-Danlos syndrome.

RISK FACTOR: Bicuspid aortic valve disease puts you at risk. If you have a bicuspid aortic valve (two leaflets instead of the typical three), or have had a bicuspid aortic valve replaced, you need to be monitored for thoracic aortic disease.

TRIGGERS: Lifestyle and trauma can trigger aortic dissection. It is possible to trigger an aortic dissection through injury to the chest, extreme straining associated with body building, illicit drug abuse, poorly controlled high blood pressure, or by discontinuing necessary blood pressure medications. On rare occasions, pregnancy can trigger an aortic dissection. However, women with aortic aneurysms and connective tissue disorders who are pregnant are at a higher risk of aortic dissection during late pregnancy and delivery and should be carefully monitored by a cardiovascular specialist.

PREVENTION: Medical management is essential to preventing aortic dissection. If you have thoracic aortic disease, medical management that includes optimal blood pressure control, aortic imaging, and genetic counseling is strongly recommended. Talk with your physician.

I know John's death will be remembered as more than the untimely end of a talented, generous man. We will look back on this tragedy as the inadvertent beginning of a movement, long in coming, dedicated to a true understanding of aortic dissection and its eventual eradication.

chapter 25

Oh Blah Dee

*T*ime heals all wounds.

There was a point when I began to doubt—make that *hate*—that old adage. Time is fickle. It doesn't "heal" wounds as much as it "salts" them. The farther down the road of grief I got, the less patience I had with myself for not having it more together.

Friends and family often smuggle unintentional, spirit-breaking smart bombs into your life. They are loaded with good intentions and the word "closure," and are cleverly engineered to annihilate you and leave everything else standing. The advice about it "being about time you got on with your life," haltingly given by someone palming the short straw they have just unfortunately drawn. The detonator is often chardonnay. Even though a thinly veiled nudge from an ad hoc itty bitty pity committee doesn't seem like it would be devastating, it is.

The only people from whom I wanted advice were other widows who had gone through and come out the other side of whatever I was experiencing at any given moment. The uncertainty about the future reminded me that a lot of the anxiety I felt stemmed from transitioning from clueless nonparent to clueless parent. Before I had a baby, I was full of eye-rolling mock and awe whenever one of my parent-friends referred to their child as nineteen or twenty-five months old, or some other seemingly random monthly breakdown. I found it annoying. *Really? A pop quiz? It was a simple question; I didn't know there'd be math.* It was hard to fathom that one-year-olds were so different from two-year-olds that, instead of just rounding up or down, every year had to be divided into twelfths. I always wanted to say, "Can you give me a rough estimate as to the age of your freaking child?"

After I had my own baby, however, the month-to-month mystery cleared up immediately. The subtle and not-so-subtle changes that are happening to your new little person can really throw you for a loop if experienced in a vacuum. Instinctively, I reached out to check my kid's progress against other kids her age. I wanted reassurance that I wasn't missing something that everyone else already knew.

Every parent who had a child even five minutes older than mine was suddenly my guru. If my baby was twenty months old, the mom with the twenty-one-month-old was Yoda. I would ask questions and then hang on every word she uttered, knowing she could see into the future. Thirty days into the future, but the future nonetheless.

The same kind of reaching out to "veterans" that eased

my mind during that transition into motherhood was what I found myself longing for after John died. I received a couple of referrals to a Web site that had blogs and bulletin boards full of postings from young widows. (I know, define "young"; I turned forty-one the day after John died, which is young in widow world.) So many of the bulletin board postings were arranged by month: "I'm four months out and it feels worse than three months, anybody else know what I'm talking about?" "What is it about eleven months? Why can't I stop crying?"

I found that chronological age has no bearing on your widow age. Twenty-year-olds counsel forty-year-olds and vice versa. The only thing that matters, the thing that we're all seeking, is finding someone farther down the road who is still standing. Whether you're up all night with the exhausting joy of a new baby or with the immobilizing shock of a never-anticipated loss, there is comfort in knowing that you're not the only one with the lights on at 2:00 a.m. wondering if you'll ever sleep again. The only way to know that this journey is survivable is to know that there are others who have actually survived it: that you're not alone in being alone.

It was heartening to know that I was not the only one for whom this fragile foray back to real life was fraught with emotional land mines. I would have to take a minute to catch up to my life every time I was blindsided by a smell, a song, or the random "it would be kind of funny if it didn't make me want to puke" moment. That first spring after we lost John, I opened the back door one morning to find John's favorite neon orange size-eleven flips-flops on the patio, poised and pointing toward our pool. They had, apparently, lain hibernating behind a potted palm all through the winter, only to announce themselves to the gardener in spring. Looking down at them, my body stood frozen and silent, while my mind scooped them up and yelled back into the house, "Hey, John, I found your shoes!" Those are the times when you realize that the overwhelming task of healing and feeling is often supported by little more than a vague survival instinct and caffeine. The most innocuous of incidents can roundhouse-kick your tenuous Bambi legs out from under you. In the widow board game, one unfortunate roll of the dice and you are picked up by the scruff of your neck and unceremoniously returned to a stage of grief from which you thought you had graduated. You are sent reeling back to square one with not so much as a "So-o-o-o-o-o-o-orry."

The thing about "closure" that I'm still grappling with most is the word itself. On paper it makes sense. The finality of coming to terms with a loss seems like an end—a closing. I get it. But for me the ongoing journey is about *opening*. I've had to open up my mind and my heart to accept, and in some cases, invent, ways to live and love and laugh that I would have never imagined myself capable of. The sensitivity that I developed after losing someone so dear to me has enhanced the way I experience my life in surprising ways. I don't know if I will ever believe in signs, but I believe in reminders. The world definitely seems full of invisible Post-it notes now, and I have imaginary strings tied on every finger. I am reminded every day to live like John would have wanted me to: all the way.

Five months after John died, I was back on a soundstage taping a TV pilot. He had always expounded on the healing effects of work therapy, and I have to say he was right. Stella was back at school and I needed a reason after dropping her off to not drive straight home and crawl back in my bed, or under it. Part of me was scared to death. I honestly didn't know if I could do it without John. For all those years, the joy I experienced when I was acting came from the anticipation of sharing every detail of my day with him.

The events of the first day should not have taken me by surprise, but they did. Crew members, not just from our show but from all over the Paramount lot, came by to share their memories of John with me. On any soundstage on any lot at any studio, you could find a dozen or so people who had worked with John and felt blessed that they had gotten the chance to do so. All week long, the production was infused with his spirit through our stories and jokes and tears. When Friday night rolled around, the audience was loaded in, the four cameras took their positions, and we were ready to roll. I was alive with the anticipation, the nerves, and the thrill that every actor longs for. My mind was in overdrive, trying to take it all in; to memorize everything—for him. An unexpected but very familiar feeling washed over me. Some things never change. I was John Ritter's window.

chapter 26

John But Not Forgotten

When John's portrait was unveiled on the side of Hollywood High, it was a day his family, friends, and fans had been anticipating for a long time. Those of us who knew him well knew that John's years at Hollywood High School were some of the happiest of his life. He never ever stopped telling the stories and reliving the glories of that time in his life. He made it very clear that being elected president of the student council as a junior, then running unopposed as a senior, were truly as thrilling to him as his Emmy, Golden Globe, or Peoples' Choice awards. Hollywood High School was where John was formed, as well as informed. Together with his best friend, Joe Landon, and his brother, Tommy, he laughed and cried and rocked and rolled himself into the person we all came to know. And love. And miss.

Muralist Elloy Torrez not only created this beautiful, heartfelt tribute to John but he and his wife, Margaret Guzman, also showed our family such kindness when we would drop by and interrupt him to gawk at the process and marvel at the scope of his vision. Elloy invited the kids to make their mark on this tribute to their father, to add that special "Ritter kid" touch. For me, seeing Stella and Jason being hoisted up on the scaffold was terrifying. They wore harnesses, but, jeez, they were suspended way the heck up there. But to witness the care they took in painting the heart with the initials of the four Ritter kids was thrilling, one of the most beautiful things I've ever seen. It will be up there forever with John.

John had an innate aptitude for appreciation, for finding that golden thread that runs through all of us and recognizing its beauty. Whether presented with one of Stella's unidentifiable half-baked art projects or with one of my unidentifiable overbaked dinners, he would always find artistry in our sincere efforts. For John, our idiosyncrasies, however flawed, were the greatest source of beauty.

I remember being very intimidated as a freshman in high school by the pottery wheel in Sister Regina's art class. Staring at a raw slab of clay, and trying to picture myself literally *turning it* into a bowl, elicited an intense fear of failure in me. I ignored, avoided, and charmed my way out of the challenging class requirement until the calendar caught up with me. With just a few weeks left to go in the school year, I was obligated to face my fear. Determined, I rolled up my sleeves and dug in. Like Michelangelo chipping away the extraneous stone to release his David from inside a marble slab, I was resolved to *will* this bowl into existence.

After days upon days of false starts and ever darkening

self-deprecating remarks, I found myself hunched over the clay once again. This time, surprisingly, I found myself actually harnessing the wheel's centrifugal force. Intuiting the correct proportions of push, pull, strength, and grace, I called upon an untapped font of patience and achieved the seemingly impossible. I made a big-ass salad bowl. No one was more surprised than I was. It was beautiful to me, a testament to the fact that I possessed a stripe of stick-to-it-iveness that was unexpected in a confirmed quitter like me.

I gently lifted my beautiful bowl onto a board and made my way with geisha-like steps across the room to the kiln. A sea of plaid-skirted pottery wheel veterans parted before me. Our beloved Sister Regina clapped her hands together and called out from behind me, "Good for you, Amy! Let's see!" I turned around much too abruptly, and watched my only successful attempt on the potter's wheel hang in the air for a moment before plunging to the floor, like Wile E. Coyote in a Road Runner cartoon. I stared at my empty board, bit my lip, and then looked down: my precious bowl. A hushed, mud-splattered class stared at me expectantly, as I took in the sight of my hard-won battle with the wheel, now just a collapsed and hopelessly warped hunk of clay. I opened my mouth to deliver the requisite joke at my own expense, but my defenses short-circuited momentarily and a sincere little sob bubbled out.

Sister Regina seized the moment. She yelled out for no one to touch it, then swooped down with a piece of wire held taut between two Popsicle sticks. Wielding her garrote like an artsy assassin, she deftly sliced my fallen masterpiece off the floor and flipped it onto another board. Sister Regina held up my twisted blob, looked at it with a huge grin, and marveled, "This is beautiful." Which is exactly what John would have said.

My life now is not what I expected when John and I fell in love. It's not what I intended, not what I was creating. Gravity took the life I imagined and added its own spin. The struggle is accepting that fact and still finding beauty and meaning in what remains.

Two years before John died—to the day, September 11, 2001—he sent Carly a letter. In it, he quoted a brilliant excerpt from one of his favorite American writers, Thornton Wilder (of *Our Town* fame). He wrote:

> *This is from his famous novel* The Bridge Over San Luis Re. *Britain's Prime Minister Tony Blair quoted a passage at a memorial service for the British citizens who were murdered in the World Trade Center attack. It is a Pulitzer Prize–winning novel written in 1928 and is a parable about the struggle to find meaning in chance and inexplicable tragedy after a bridge collapses in Peru, killing five people:*

> *But soon we will die, and all memories of those five will have left Earth, and we ourselves shall be loved for a while and forgotten. But the love will have been enough; all those impulses of love return to the love that made them. Even memory is not necessary for love.*

There is a land of the living in a land of the dead and the bridge is love. The only survival, the only meaning.

John knew then, as I know now, that what remains is love. And no one loved him more than his family.

I remember writing to Carly when she first went back to Vassar after the funeral. I told her that I felt a kind of—beware of Catholic references ahead—communion with her dad through her. There was so much sadness on top of us and so much more coming. I knew that in the days ahead another throat punch or two were waiting for me around the corner. But I found a kind of peace in talking to Carly. We felt like we had been somehow ejected from our home planet. We were lost in space, and talking about our home was so important because we never wanted to forget where we came from and that it was real. Carly and I agreed that, in large part, her dad had made us who we are, as if things only became real when we told John about them. We needed to constantly remember that he would have hated for us to stop *becoming* just because he was not here. It's important to keep doing what would've cracked him up, blown his mind, and made him proud, because it's the funny, mind-blowing, proud way to live. He had the secret of life and he shared it with everybody—and it was designed and intended to sustain us daily and forever. Amen.

I obviously can't go to him for advice anymore. I have to call upon conversations and stories from our life together to create dialogues about everyday things going on without him in the present. The comfort of having someone to "check in with" is just gone, and you can't really understand the value of having that in your life until you've lost it—particularly when it comes to raising a child.

I remember us driving around Albany, New York, in the middle of winter when Stella was two. She had never seen snow before, so we decided to get sleds and conquer the slopes of the local snow-covered, abandoned-for-the-season golf course. Forgive us our trespasses. We got out of our car with Stella and saucers in tow and walked across about a quarter acre of what were tees, sand traps, and greens for most of the year. For us, this sparkling winter day was our private winter wonderland. Then I saw the hill. More like a cliff. It seemed to drop straight down from where we were standing.

Now, I'm a bit of a thrill-seeker; under controlled circumstances, I've proven myself undaunted by heights, roller coasters, or flying in F-18s. However, throwing caution to the wind is one thing, throwing your daughter down a hill is quite another. John was always brave about letting Stella do things, but I was a very cautious mom. Stella was my first kid and his fourth, so he'd seen it all by then. As I took in the magnitude of the drop, I kept saying, "Is this okay? This is okay, right?" He said, "There's like an eighty percent chance she'll live." Through gritted teeth I could only respond: "That's not even funny."

Just when he thought it couldn't get any chillier, he explained, "I only say that stuff because you're obsessing with the possibility that something bad might happen. And really, what are the chances of that? Twenty percent, maybe? Those are good odds . . . soooo . . . here we go!" I didn't budge.

We stood at the precipice debating our divergent child-rearing philosophies; mine was brand-new and flawed, his was old and jaded. Stella, shivering in my arms, kept glancing back and forth between the hill and the car. Finally, sensing a standoff, he gave up hope of swaying me with his line of reasoning and pulled a Nike: "Don't think about it, just do it!" And with that, he hopped on his saucer and awkwardly pushed off with one boot. The off-kilter kick-start had rotated his saucer 180 degrees. We watched his face as he plummeted with wild exhilaration, laughing and mugging all the way down the hill. Once at the bottom, he looked up at us with his arms outstretched and his beard encrusted with snow, shouting up to us "Come to Papa!" As usual, his joy was irresistible.

I sat Stella down in front of me, held her tight, and pushed off. Hurtling down the hill, I felt her breath catch with elation as she leaned back against me, thrilled. Picking up speed as we went, we were two objects in motion being drawn to the center of our universe. A mere five feet in front of John, our saucer came to an abrupt halt. Compelled by the combined unstoppable forces of momentum and love, Stella flew into her father's arms. And it was beautiful.

John's philosophy of loosening the reins a bit and letting kids experience life turned out to be the theme of that great Disney movie *Finding Nemo*. We saw it with Stella the summer before John died, but it wasn't until I watched it again recently that the full impact of that theme struck home. The reason the dad fish (played by Albert Brooks) is so protective, is that the mom fish unexpectedly died and he's alone with this adventurous little kid. Hello-o? I was the dad fish now. I had never been a free-reign kind of mom, but now my "unfounded trepidation" seemed validated. Mortality was staring me right in the face, confirming that bad things can happen at any moment. John's opposite point of view—his yin to my yang—was that this could be your last day to have fun. He's not around to remind me of that anymore, but his absence is reminder enough. Now, more than ever, I have to teach Stella to be fearless even though I, myself, on occasion, am racked with fear.

I've been working on appropriating his *carpe diem* approach to life in the way I live mine, especially when it comes to raising Stella. His voice still rings in my ears as I suppress the urge to hover, assuring me that she'll never know the scope of her abilities unless she's given the chance to screw things up royally. Stella reminds me, too. With humor of course. In her five years with her father she observed and absorbed his spirit. She learned early and well that *making light* is sometimes the best way to *shed light*.

John approached every situation—mundane, joyous, or sad—with humor. It was the first and finest tool in his box; his spirit of comedy was the very core of who he was as a person. That was one of the philosophies we shared: that laughter is the best medicine. John's sense of fun and mischief informed everything he did; he communicated with everyone through laughter, and he did it with love. Always. Of all the wonderful things that have been said about him,

I think this sums it up best: "If everybody who loves John would just go out there every day and do two things—do one really nice thing for someone, and then do something really goofy—I think that would make John really happy." Strengthening and nurturing our connectedness, with love and laughter, was the John Ritter way.

Acknowledgments

Thanks to Tricia Boczkowski, Peter Higgins, Jay Ginsberg, Steven Weber, Mike Zilliox, Joe Landon, Bob Myman, Michael Plonsker, Jennifer Grega, Beverly Borine, Jenn Vacirca, Sissy Slayton, and Carly Ritter for encouraging me to birth this baby naturally (without the use of a ghostwriter or an epidural) and then actually holding my hand and reminding me to breathe during two years of labor.

Thanks to Yas/zbeck and Ritter kin near and far for the ongoing love and support you have given to Stella and to me.

Thanks to Kelly Phelan and Ken Bracken for being the teachers I've always wanted.

Most important: Thank you to John for all those years of saying, "You should be writing this stuff down." I finally heard you . . .

Printed in the United States
By Bookmasters